VISUAL CRIMINOLOGY

Bill McClanahan

BRISTOL
UNIVERSITY
PRESS

New Horizons in Criminology series

Series Editor: **Andrew Millie**,
Edge Hill University, UK

New Horizons in Criminology series provides concise, authoritative texts which reflect cutting-edge thought and theoretical development with an international scope. Written by leading authors in their fields, the series has become essential reading for all academics and students interested in where criminology is heading.

Forthcoming in the series:

Redemptive Criminology
Aaron Pycroft and **Clemens Bartollas**

Out now in the series:

A Criminology Of Narrative Fiction
Rafe McGregor

Transnational Criminology:
Trafficking and Global Criminal Markets
Simon Mackenzie

Wildlife Criminology
Angus Nurse and **Tanya Wyatt**

Find out more at
bristoluniversitypress.co.uk/new-horizons-in-criminology

First published in Great Britain in 2023 by

Bristol University Press
University of Bristol
1-9 Old Park Hill
Bristol
BS2 8BB
UK
t: +44 (0)117 374 6645
e: bup-info@bristol.ac.uk

Details of international sales and distribution partners are available at bristoluniversitypress.co.uk

British Library Cataloguing in Publication Data
A catalogue record for this book is available from the British Library

ISBN 978-1-5292-0744-6 hardcover
ISBN 978-1-5292-0745-3 paperback
ISBN 978-1-5292-0747-7 ePub
ISBN 978-1-5292-0746-0 ePdf

Cover design: Dave Worth
Front cover image: Eric Brittain

Bristol University Press uses environmentally responsible print partners.

Contents

List of Figures

About the Author

Bill McClanahan is Assistant Professor of Justice Studies in the School of Justice Studies at Eastern Kentucky University in Richmond, KY. His research and writing on ecology, visual cultures, and police has appeared in a number of academic journals and other venues, and he is coauthor (with Avi Brisman, Nigel South, and Reece Walters) of *Water, Crime and Security in the Twenty-First Century: Too Dirty, Too Little, Too Much* (Palgrave, 2018).

Acknowledgements

Thanks to all of the creative thinkers who gave this book a reason to be written. Thanks particularly to Travis Linnemann, Judah Schept, and Tyler Wall, who have all offered immeasurably helpful feedback here and everywhere else. Thanks to my friends at Eastern Kentucky University, especially Avi Brisman, Victoria Collins, and Doug Peach for their insightful support and gracious friendship. The same goes for Katherine Biber, Eric Brittain, Michelle Brown, Eamonn Carrabine, Lorenzo Natali, and Nigel South, who have all offered support, inspiration, insight, and friendship. Finally, to Nicole Rafter, whose warmth and brilliance animate whatever good material readers may find here.

I would like to thank the staff at Bristol University Press for their kind assistance and patience, as well as Andrew Millie, who invited me to contribute to this series and whose help has been instrumental, and all of the artists and photographers who kindly granted permission for me to use their work.

Thanks also to my mom, Cia White, and my sister, Annie McClanahan, along with the rest of my family. Last but never least, to Tatiana Sanchez Parra. This book, like everything else, was made possible only by her love and companionship.

NEW HORIZONS IN CRIMINOLOGY

Series editor: Professor Andrew Millie, Department of Law and Criminology, Edge Hill University, UK

Preface

The New Horizons in Criminology series aims to provide high quality and authoritative texts which reflect cutting-edge thought and theoretical development in criminology. All books are international in scope and are accessible and concise. One of the most exciting 'new horizons' to emerge in the last 10–15 years has been visual criminology and I was delighted when Bill McClanahan agreed to contribute this text. His work is always worth reading and pushes the boundaries of criminological thinking, whether on green criminology, rural criminology or visual criminology (e.g. McClanahan 2014; Brisman et al 2018; McClanahan and Linnemann 2018). When I was shown the first draft of this book I was very impressed. His writing is clear, accessible and engaging and this ought to become the go-to book for visual criminology.

In the book McClanahan traces the origins of visual criminology in the various forms of visual sociology, anthropology and visual studies. He also considers the scope for visual methods within criminology. According to Nicole Rafter (2014: 129) visual criminology is 'the study of ways in which all things visual interact with crime and criminal justice, inventing and shaping one another'. This reciprocal relationship between images and our understandings of crime and justice is central to visual criminology; as McClanahan highlights, this is not a criminology *with* images, using images merely for illustration. Rather, the visual is an important element in our construction and interpretation of crime, criminal justice systems and social harms. There are clear examples where the visual ought to be of criminological interest, be it the orange jumpsuits of Guantanamo Bay prisoners, the architecture of confinement, the proliferation of cop shows and docudramas on our TVs, or perhaps the sight of a police car speeding through a community with lights flashing and siren wailing. In this last example, it may be our engagement with sound as well as the visual that aids our construction of policing. McClanahan is aware that privileging the visual over other sensory engagement may lead to 'ocularcentrism', and in his work with Nigel South he has suggested scope for a sensory criminology (2020), also considered here. Yet it is the visual that dominates, as demonstrated by the example used by McClanahan to start this book.

The book begins with the murder of George Floyd in May 2020, by a police officer with his knees on Floyd's neck and back. As McClanahan highlights, 'The murder was captured, like so many are now, by the mobile phone cameras of bystanders'. These images spread rapidly around the world leading to protests and violence on streets far removed from the original incident in Minneapolis, Minnesota. The original images—and others related to this case—in many ways, took on extra meanings and interpretations as they were reproduced in different contexts.

The importance of the visual in constructions of policing is the concern of Chapter 7 of this book. By itself, this chapter is an important contribution to criminology; yet the book offers much more. Elsewhere in Chapter 4, by drawing on green criminology, McClanahan considers the visual in relation to environmental harms. In Chapter 5 the influence of the visual to our understandings of drugs and drugs culture is explored, and 'the ways in which drug images contributed to global trends in mass incarceration and policing'. Following this in Chapter 6, the focus is punishment, prisons, and the visual, with special focus on 'the role of the image in constructing and communicating a carceral culture'.

The book's concluding chapter considers the future for a visual criminology; as McClanahan notes, 'it seems we will continue to meet spectacle with gaze'. This book makes a significant contribution to our understandings of relationships between the visual and crime, justice and social harm. I certainly recommend it to students and academics interested in visual criminology. However, my hope is that it will have broader impact—and not just within criminology. The book has certainly influenced my thinking and has the potential to become an important text.

References

Brisman, A., McClanahan, B., South, N., and Walters, R. (2018). *Water, Crime and Security in the Twenty-First Century: Too Dirty, Too Little, Too Much*. Basingstoke: Palgrave Macmillan.

McClanahan, B. (2014). Green and grey: Water justice, criminalization, and resistance. *Critical Criminology*, 22(3), 403–18.

McClanahan, B. and Linnemann, T. (2018). Darkness on the edge of town: Visual criminology and the 'black sites' of the rural. *Deviant Behavior*, 39(4), 512–24.

McClanahan, B. and South, N. (2020) 'All knowledge begins with the senses': Towards a sensory criminology. *British Journal of Criminology*, 60(1), 3–23.

Rafter, N. (2014). Introduction to special issue on visual culture and the iconography of crime and punishment. *Theoretical Criminology*, 18(2), 127–33.

1

Introducing Visual Criminology

Introduction

On the afternoon of 25 May 2020, police in Minneapolis, Minnesota approached George Floyd, an unarmed 46-year-old Black man, following a tip that Floyd had attempted to pass a counterfeit $20 note to a store clerk. During the interaction, a white cop, Derek Chauvin, detained George Floyd on the pavement with his knees on Floyd's neck and back as a physically passive Floyd struggled to breath. For nearly nine minutes, Chauvin—with the assistance of three other cops—remained on top of George Floyd, ultimately killing him. The murder was captured, like so many are now, by the mobile phone cameras of bystanders, and by the next day the footage had circulated internationally. Almost immediately, global protests against police violence began, focusing largely on George Floyd and Breonna Taylor, a Black woman murdered in her home by police, two weeks prior to Floyd, in my own hometown of Louisville, Kentucky. At the time of this writing, almost six months later, those protests continue in every major American city and around the world, and George Floyd and Breonna Taylor are the tragic symbols, their names hoarsely shouted and spray painted, their faces appearing on placards and signs and shirts and murals.

The image of Chauvin with his knee on the neck of a dying George Floyd, it seems to me, is the essential criminological image of the contemporary moment. I do not reproduce it here, not because it is too shocking—American police murdering an unarmed Black man should not, by now, come as a shock to anyone—but because it is too familiar. We know what it looks like when police murder. We know the familiar aesthetic qualities of the bodycam and the furtively filmed bystander cell phone video, just as we know all too well the carefully choreographed performance of outrage and reform that inevitably follows each murder. We do not need to see it here, again. As we shall see, the visual criminology that gives this book life is not simply a criminology of images, and so I have no interest in following it towards an exhaustive analysis of the composition of the already iconic image

Figure 1.1: A mural of George Floyd on the Israeli separation wall in Bethlehem, West Bank

Source: Courtesy of Imago Images/UPI Photo.

of Floyd's killing. Instead of that painfully familiar image of George Floyd, then, let us consider one that might not be as settled.

George Floyd is not, here, being coldly murdered by police. He is not on the ground, with cop Derek Chauvin's knee in his neck as he pleads for his mother or utters the same dying words, "I can't breathe", as other victims of police strangulation like Eric Garner and all of the other people whose names we do not know so well but who also died struggling to breathe at the hands and knees of police. He is not even, in this image, grounded within the American context in which we began. Instead, George Floyd's solemn face and the name of his hometown of Houston, Texas are rendered on the separation wall that divides the occupied West Bank in Palestinian Bethlehem, some 6,000 miles away from the Powderhorn Park neighborhood of Minneapolis where he was killed. The wall, of course, is itself an intensely visible and visual technology of racist power and violence, and it is surely a sign of the power of the image that Floyd's murder was immediately understood by West Bank residents as an exercise of the same global logics and power that built the wall, and so of course his face was painted there. George Floyd's face would ultimately appear several times in different murals on the separation wall (as would the faces of other victims of police violence from around the world), where *his* memory would come to be put into service by activists alongside the memory of Eyad al-Hallaq, a 32-year-old Palestinian man murdered by Israeli police in Jerusalem just five days after George Floyd was killed in Minnesota. By July of 2020, Eyad al-Hallaq's name was also being chanted, alongside George Floyd's and Breonna Taylor's, his face appearing on signs carried by demonstrators in the US and around the world.

What does it mean, then, to have these images, and all the other images we have of crime, harm, and justice? What do we make of and do with all of the criminological images that surround us? What does it mean or demonstrate that we have such a robust international corpus of film of police murder? What does it mean that while some of us saw the video of George Floyd's killing and felt, as much as we could, the suffering and sadness and pain and violence that made the whole event what it was and reacted with appropriately heartbroken outrage, others saw a defensible and acceptable application of police power? Months after the murder, moreover, Minneapolis police made public the footage of the event recorded on police body-worn cameras, and some viewers found in that new footage the opportunity to rehabilitate the image of police from a growing public backlash, deciding that the new footage largely exonerated the cops. What does it mean, for that matter, to live in conditions in which the only hope for justice for those killed by police and state violence, is that someone will have happened along and captured a killing on camera? Why do we both demand and question visual evidence, even when the moment in question is as quotidian and familiar as the killing of a Black man by a cop, and what does that say about how we take in and know the world that we need to keep seeing it? Finally, what does it mean to see the image of a murder and its victim travel so quickly around the world, shared on digital platforms and painted on separation walls and broadcast on the nightly news and haunting our dreams, and to see that image and the moments and processes it implicates explode at the center of a global struggle?

The visual in visual criminology, these questions remind us, is as much about the moments and contexts of production as the images themselves; as I will argue throughout the book, visual criminology is interested in processes and events, not simply pictures. What historical and political processes put George Floyd on the ground, or put Chauvin's knee in his neck? When the faces and names of George Floyd and Breonna Taylor and Eyad al-Hallaq started appearing on protest signs around the world, or when a subset of the viewing public saw nothing wrong in the images of Floyd's killing? These are the sorts of questions that this book responds to, and these are all the sorts of questions that should remain at the core of a critical visual criminology.

Gazing and seeing

When we saw those first images of George Floyd and the cops that killed him, and then later when we saw his face appearing on the walls of the occupied West Bank, we did what we always do: we looked. It was, of course, all we could ever do. As sighted beings, we move through the world visually, taking in troves of information every moment. Unsighted, we gaze into and from the mind's eye. In the particular moments in which George Floyd's face and name came into public consciousness, we were particularly primed to gaze at visual media, too, as most of us had only recently largely retreated into our homes in the face of the COVID-19 pandemic that began early in the year: most of us, no matter where we were in the early months of 2020, were spending most of our time looking at images on our televisions and our phones and computers.

As social scientists, too, we are already uniquely oriented to the concept of gazing and seeing; everyone from Mills to Foucault, each of the canonical authors and thinkers and theorists we all read and recognize as forebears, understood the enterprise of social analysis to be one founded on looking. Our other senses play their important roles, but it seems that at the end of the day, the eyes have it. The sociological gaze—the process that provides the optical inputs that inform what Mills (1959) called 'the sociological imagination'—then, is in some sense the starting point for all methods and modes of analysis, less a single moment than a series of moments in which interest is piqued, questions are raised, and answers are sought.

Criminology is no exception. We have known all along that criminology has its own eyes, its own windows to peer out of and into. What matters most here is not, though, what that gaze lands on. Instead, it is the act of gazing itself—that practice and process we undertook when we took in George Floyd on the ground, for example, or on the wall, or when we saw his name and face on memorials and protest signs around the world, from Australia to Zimbabwe, as part of an articulation of Black life and pain—that most informs this book and visual criminology as an emergent field. In order to adequately respond to Eamonn Carrabine's (2012: 463) calls for a criminological perspective and agenda that is equipped to make sense of what he calls 'the ascendant power of spectacle' in the contemporary world, criminology must take inventory of its optical tools and tendencies, and must begin to consider the potential and pitfalls that are likely to emerge. Criminology must also, though, reckon not only with the plain fact that it is largely a study of power, and that seeing, gazing, vision, and visualization are practices that all imply or implicate power, but also that criminology's own ways of seeing have contributed significantly to the violence, inequality, harm, and oppression that make up 'criminal justice' wherever it comes into being.

The criminologically compelling thing about the images of George Floyd discussed and reproduced here is not that they offer us some new vantage point from which to see or know the violence of police, or from which to better or more fully understand the ways in which race and class condition justice; sadly, they only reproduce a familiar scene and a familiar vantage point, and we all know exactly what it looks like, optically, when police kill their prey. Instead, the utility of these images for a visual criminology—and, I think, for a more critical understanding of the social world—is in questions surrounding the much broader contexts of their production, their circulation, and their reception.

Introducing visual criminology

Visual criminology formally came about, in the mid-2010s, in a time in which it seems like there was no choice; as Michelle Brown and Carrabine note, the field emerged in and from 'the context of an unprecedented proliferation of images, sites of production, and modes of analysis' (2017: 1), a 'time defined by the spectacular proliferation of media' (2019: 191). Or, to put it another way: there are always more and more images, and visual criminology is one among more and more ways of seeing.

While there had already been some prior meaningful criminological engagement with images and the visual, visual criminology proper—as a distinct, named, and delineated field of study—more or less formally came into being with the 2014 publication of a special issue on 'Visual Culture and the Iconography of Crime and Punishment' of the journal *Theoretical Criminology* edited by Nicole Rafter. In the introduction to that issue, Rafter (2014: 129) offers the foundational definition and description of visual criminology: 'visual criminology is the study of ways in which all things visual interact with crime and criminal justice, inventing and shaping one another'. Rafter also notes that criminology has obviously already engaged with media, but joins cultural criminologists Hayward and Presdee, who in 2010 (2) argued that a new criminological 'orientation' should move beyond 'disciplinary drift into the realm of the image' that, in these authors' view, would 'hardly constitute an adequate visual criminology'. A year prior to that, Hayward also sketched a brief outline of a distinctly visual cultural criminology, although, as described later in this chapter, that effort was more focused on cultural criminology's longstanding interest in mediated spectacles of crime than it was on the sort of processual and conceptual concerns that would ultimately constitute a visual criminology.

While the 2014 special issue of *Theoretical Criminology* marks the formal starting point of visual criminology, the seeds for its development had been sewn earlier across a number of criminological tendencies and disciplines. Most notably, early signs of a visual tendency emerged in critical criminological streams like cultural criminology, which had always made an engagement with the visual a central plank in its platform. Because the 'visual' in visual criminology points, just as in the fields of visual cultures and visual studies, to an unfixed set of processes and practices (see generally Young 2014; Knauss and Pezzoli-Olgiati 2015: 2; Carrabine 2017; Natali and McClanahan 2017, 2020) including visualization and other non-optical and imaginative ways of seeing, it is in some sense a natural companion with cultural criminology, which was itself partly inspired by an interest in the idea of a criminological imagination and an interest in the ways in which crime is imagined and given meaning and significance. Many of the concepts and theorists most engaged with by visual criminology—for example, early- and mid-century social theory associated with formations like the Frankfurt School of critical theory (particularly Walter Benjamin and Theodor Adorno's respective work on the forces that condition cultural production) and the French Situationist movement (particularly Guy Debord's work on 'spectacle' as the governing conceptual architecture of contemporary social life, relations, and organization)—had already been lurking in the bibliographies of critical and cultural criminology.[1] This is a condition of which cultural criminologists have long been keenly aware, with Jeff Ferrell and Cecile Van de Voorde (2010: 36) noting that the field had reached a 'decisive moment' in which there was no choice but to account for the visual as a process and practice and site in which crime, harm, and justice are constituted.

Examples of the visual tendency—in the same form we would expect to find it today—in cultural criminology include *Judging the Image* (2005), in which criminologist Alison Young describes various relations between art, jurisprudence, legal theory and law, and crime, and *Culture of Punishment* (2009), in which Michelle Brown

6

traces the cultural shape of mass incarceration through, among other cultural productions, the image and cinema. Later, Rafter and Brown coauthored *Criminology Goes to the Movies* (2011), a collection of essays analyzing cinema through criminological lenses and demonstrating, along the way, a deeply visual form of the sort of 'popular criminology' that informed most of Rafter's work on visual criminology. Work by other criminologists like Ferrell, Young, and others, meanwhile, had long turned the criminological gaze towards the image, most notably through an interest in graffiti and street art (see generally Ferrell 1993, 1995; Halsey and Young 2002, 2006; Alvelos 2004; Snyder 2006, 2011; Young 2014). More recently, Rafe McGregor has proposed 'a criminology of narrative fiction', which argues for the 'criminological value of fiction' including 'cinematic fictions' in part precisely because those cinematic narratives reach large audiences, further underscoring the intersections of narrative, popular, and visual criminologies (McGregor 2020: 13).

The visual tendency in cultural criminology is made most clear, though, in 2010's *Framing Crime*, edited by Keith Hayward and the late Mike Presdee. In this influential collection, a handful of cultural criminologists demonstrate the visual tendency in essays on a remarkably diverse list of topics including state executions, sports violence, car commercials, and punishment regimes. In the introduction to this volume, Hayward (2010) reiterates the concern of cultural criminology with the cultural processes that produce crime and, importantly, the meanings we attach to crime. Generally anticipating some of the elemental concerns of the soon to emerge visual criminology, Hayward describes the proliferation of images— obviously not a prophetic observation in the digital 21st century, but an important one nevertheless—and the reductive conflation of 'image' and 'visual' as problems for analysis.

We might also simply imagine visual criminology as a contemporary variant of critical criminology, the broader contextual field that serves as the umbrella orientation over a host of related and comingling orientations. This relationship to the critical tradition in criminology has significantly shaped the contours of visual criminology, drawing it into conversation with other critical concentrations including human–environment relations (Natali 2010, 2016; Natali and McClanahan 2017, 2020), prisons (Fiddler 2007; Jewkes and Johnson 2007; Carrabine 2010, 2019; Brown 2014; Schept 2014; Schept and Frank 2015; Jewkes and Moran 2017), police (Wall and Linnemann 2014; Linnemann 2016, 2017a; Wall 2019), and more. Brown and Carrabine (2019: 192), in describing the critical foundations of visual criminology, underscore this tendency in visual criminology by noting that 'visual criminology echoes the activism and opposition to mainstream forms of consensus and classical criminology'.

Visual criminology also maintains its relationship to critical criminologies by taking seriously the intersecting problems of race, class, gender, and sexuality. In particular, the visual tendency in criminology has produced significant critical research on the intertwined dynamics of gender and crime (Dirks 2004; Dirks et al 2015; Zack et al 2018) and race, racialization, and crime (Biber 2007; Linnemann and Kurtz 2014).

Finally, visual criminology as it stands today, despite my claims surrounding a focus on processes and conditioning factors rather than individual optical images, does retain a real and useful interest in what we can imagine as criminological images. Like the images of the police murder of George Floyd discussed at the outset, these are the images we can interrogate for some useful insight into the relational processes that condition the coproduction of harm, crime, or justice and the image and its reception. These might be popular or well-known images such as the killing of Floyd, artistic productions like the photographs of Diane Arbus (Carrabine 2012), administrative images like evidentiary images and textual documents (Biber 2013, 2018), images produced in service of police power (Wall 2019), historical non-image archival materials like three-dimensional material ecological artefacts (McClanahan 2017), popular media including cinema and television (Wakeman 2014, 2018; Rafter and Brown 2011; Kohm and Greenhill 2011; McClanahan et al 2017), and a host of other artistic, commercial, cinematic, and digital visual images. What matters most, for a robust visual criminology, is that when they are included, images be approached as something more than illustrative window dressing, a process that Alison Young (2014) describes as shifting the image from 'object to encounter', a theme and point of guidance taken up again in the next section and then revisited throughout the book. For me, then, a visual criminology is at play whenever that shift is undertaken in the analysis of the visual dimensions of crime, harm, and justice.

Visual criminology: themes and developments

Fast forwarding from the early and mid-2000s and 2010s to today, we find a visual criminology that is far more fully formed, and far less protozoic. Following 2014, those pursuing the sort of visual analysis generally prescribed by visual criminology had a banner under which to situate their work, and older examples of the visual criminological tendency could be understood retroactively through the new lenses offered by an expressly and overtly visual criminology. Given the ongoing proliferation of the visual, and the ways in which it seems that proliferation is intensifying in scope and power exponentially with each passing moment, it stands to reason that visual criminology is a fast-moving and rapidly growing area. Here, I briefly sketch an outline of some of notable moments in which we have seen visual criminology come to life.

One particular area in which visual criminology has thrived is green criminology, a field that emerged like visual criminology, although some years earlier, from critical and cultural criminologies and one that focuses its criminological gaze on environmental harms and crimes and human–environment relations. Green criminology has seen sustained calls for the development of an explicitly visual criminological tendency in the field (see generally, for example, Natali 2010, 2016; Natali and McClanahan 2017, 2020). In his most direct contribution to green criminology, cultural criminologist Jeff Ferrell also noted the potential in both a visual and a green-visual criminology, claiming that 'among cultural criminology's more useful innovations has been its emphasis on the visual' and that 'a visual criminology of this sort seems particularly appropriate for recording and communicating the little lost ecologies of everyday life' (Ferrell 2013: 360). Indeed, the intersections of green and cultural criminology described by Avi Brisman and Nigel South (2013, 2014) seems a particularly fruitful site of ongoing visual criminological analysis. Finally, climate change—the biggest challenge facing not only criminology but all planetary existence (Bendell 2018; White 2018a)—has enlivened the visual imagination of green criminology, with ongoing efforts to understand the mediated dimensions of the problem (Lam and Tegelberg 2020) and to grapple with the ways in which climate change implicates the practices of visualization and optical vision (Brisman 2014, 2015).

Visual criminology has also asserted on to critical criminology a more full and contemporary account of race and its role in the social worlds of crime, harm, and justice. Racial difference is, after all, more visual than scientific, and Katherine Biber (2007: 45) has described the ways in which law, with all of its power to construct truth, continues to understand race as a 'visual genre'. Visually minded criminologists have responded to the entangled issues of race and the visual, often considering the ways in which crime and justice are conditioned by racialized images. Much of the explicit criminological interest in this area, though, is illustrative of an approach informed more by a qualitative media analysis that is chiefly concerned with issues of representation rather than with the broader concerns and interests of visual criminology proper (see generally Eigenberg and Park 2016; Park et al 2018; Glover 2019). Others, like Biber, working more explicitly in the area of visual criminology, though, have also undertaken projects that consider the processes of the visual more comprehensively in order to reckon with the role of the image in the always-entangled practices of racialization and criminalization.

Like race, gender is also a social dynamic and condition that has attracted some significant consideration from visually minded criminologists who have made important contributions to our understanding of the ways in which gender functions in and across visual cultures of crime and justice. These include work that provides criminological insight into the ways in which feminist readings of wartime images challenge important temporal and spatial distinctions (Walklate 2018: 617) and work that considers the ways in which subjective experiences of incarceration are configured and conditioned by gender (Dirks et al 2015). There has also been some sustained effort, in visual criminology, to better account for the role of gender in methodological decision making, too. Here, visual criminologists have made important contributions to the ways in which the broader discipline might develop methodological approaches that are more attentive to the various ways that gender conditions the social worlds of crime and justice (Fitzgibbon and Stengel 2018).

As represented and described in Chapter 5 of this book, the visual tendency in criminology has also made significant contributions to the ways in which we think criminologically about the moments in which harm, crime, and justice intersect with the lived and visible worlds of criminalized drugs and drug users. It makes sense that criminologists would note and take interest in the vast body of drug images that surround us; drugs, after all, are at the heart of some of the most visible and noteworthy moments in crime and justice. Largely thanks to the relationship between drugs and policing and punishment, the ways in which drug images configure our perceptions of crime and justice are crystal clear and insistently visual and visible. Important contributions to the visual criminology of drugs include research that uses photo-ethnographic methods (Copes et al 2018b) and work that describes the role of the visual dimensions of drug addiction in the construction of racial difference (Linnemann and Wall 2013).

Among the various forms of the image and visual work that have captivated and sustained the attention of visual criminologists, perhaps none is more steadfast in its relation to the critical criminological enterprise than graffiti and 'street art'. At the heart of a virtual trove of critical and, quite consistently, *visual* criminology is an interest in the ways in which the illicit images of graffiti function, move, and make meaning in and of the social and material world. Although this work is not always representative of the careful attention given by visual criminology proper to the processual and relational dimensions of the image and its production, and while it also sometimes seems to risk obscuring any critical insights behind the aestheticization of transgressive visual culture, it is all the same ample evidence of a special relationship between critical criminologies (including cultural and visual varieties) and the visual worlds of graffiti and street art. Work in this area of criminology has considered everything from the dynamics of criminalization and tensions between subcultural and dominant forms of success (Snyder 2006, 2011) to the ways in which graffiti structures the material organization of the city and the affective experience of producing or encountering graffiti (Halsey and Young 2006; Young 2012, 2014), to the affective experience of producing graffiti (Ferrell 1995).

Visually inclined criminologists and those working explicitly in the area of visual criminology have also made significant contributions to the ways in which visual research is done. As described later, in Chapter 3, visual criminology is undertaken through distinct methodological formations, and any serious consideration of the development of the field (but also of contemporary visual research more broadly) should take these contributions into account. Methodological techniques and approaches pioneered and refined by visual criminologists include the production of images in the field (see generally Natali and McClanahan 2017, 2020; Copes et al 2018a, 2018b, 2019), the use of photo-elicitation interviewing (see generally Natali and McClanahan 2017), the critical and qualitative systematic analysis of images (see generally Natali and McClanahan 2017), and perhaps most notably and inventively, the use of documentary filmmaking techniques (see generally Hayward 2017; Redmon 2017, 2018).

Finally, and perhaps most notably, a robust visual criminology has coalesced around the critical study of prisons, punishment, and the tendencies of the carceral state. Punishment, it seems, lends itself exceptionally well to visual thinking; prisons and jails, after all, are distinct spaces with distinct aesthetics and spatial-cultural meaning and significance, unique architectures, and distinct visual cultures of their own. The material spaces of punishment, moreover, are deeply suggestive of the acts of looking and seeing, and of the power of 'visuality', discussed more thoroughly in the next chapter. As Rafter suggests and Kate West (2017) describes, the origins of the visual tendency in criminology are most evident in Cesare Lombroso, whose own work, to quote West (2017: 273), was often 'entirely composed of … images'. While it might seem odd that a critical, sociological, and sometimes even polemical stream of scholarship would eventually develop from arch positivist Lombroso, who also inspired biological and early biosocial criminologies,[2] the fundamental relation in his work between the visual and the logics and spaces of punishment is clear: working in the latter half of the 19th century at Turin in Italy, Lombroso's interest was in the physiognomy of the criminally insane, and it was there that he developed his theory of criminal atavism based largely on the classification of individuals by way of visible physiognomic features. Lombroso's work in this area would be foundational in criminology writ large,[3] but is particularly useful here simply as evidence of the enduring desire for a visually guided criminology. Lombroso's interest in the image was not, however, limited to the images of atavistic criminals he is most known for; he also maintained, throughout his career, a strong interest in the art of psychiatric patients, art for which Lombroso, true to his character, attempted to develop a rigid system of classification. From the Lombrosian interest in the physical appearance of 'criminal man' to the elemental panopticism of the prison, it seems as though the visual tendency in criminology is plainly evident in research on prisons, punishment, and carcerality.

What visual criminology isn't

For all of this talk of what visual criminology is, it also requires an anti-definition: what we imagine when we first hear the phrase is, more often than not, not what is meant. Encountering the term 'visual criminology', there is a temptation to take it to mean a criminology that is presented visually. While there are ample examples of exactly that, and while many of those examples are also visual criminology proper, it's nevertheless the case that simply making criminology visible does not make a visual criminology. Rather than simply *being* visual, as described here and throughout, visual criminology is *about* the visual.

Similarly, there are many streams of criminology that have already demonstrated an interest in engaging with images, but all the same are *not* visual criminology. Cultural criminology as described earlier, for example, has often included and engaged with images, most notably in the form of the pictures produced by social movements (see, for example, McClanahan 2014) and criminal(ized) subcultures (see generally Ferrell 1995). This tendency, though, does not constitute a visual criminology, but instead something like a 'criminology with images' (Natali and McClanahan 2020).

Criminologist and critic Phil Carney gets beautifully to the heart of this important distinction, albeit in a way that is somewhat limited to the photographic image, by suggesting that we 'conceive of photography as a kind of material force in itself', a 'heavy vapour … oozing out of machines, swirling around and buffeting the bodies of spectators and spectated' (2017: 281). What Carney suggests here is the essential point that underpins visual criminology: rather than imagining the limits of the visual as the discreet image-objects of pictures, we should instead imagine it as far more elemental and often, in fact, *invisible*, as suggested by Carney's notion of swirling vapor, a pleasantly evocative way in which to orient our thinking and, yes, our gazing.

Importantly, visual criminology is not simply the criminological study of media and mediated images. While media is certainly important for visual criminology, and while mediated images are centrally important in many examples of visual criminology, it is not simply a criminology of media. There have been several moments of serious criminological engagement with media as a field and a force (see generally Jewkes and Linnemann 2017), and while these inform and presage plenty of visual criminology proper, they are not synonymous; the concerns and interests of visual criminology are significantly broader than a focus on 'media' would suggest.

Returning to Young (2014: 159), visual criminology is attentive to the image in ways that allow the visual to be understood as having a 'dynamic role … in the constitution of crime in contemporary society and culture, thanks to the affective dimension of the encounter between spectator and image'. This again is the essential distinction between visual criminology and a criminology with images, characterized by a tendency to construct images 'as objects of analysis rather than as constitutive elements of the discursive field' (Young 2014: 159). Rather than the marginal images produced by the image-as-object tendency, the visual criminology described here and elsewhere seeks to conceptualize the political, historical, social, and material forces that not only condition but also constitute our everyday encounters with the spectacles of crime, harm, and justice.

Finally, before describing what this book is and what it aims to do, some brief notes on what it is *not*. Most significantly, it is not comprehensive; a full accounting of the visual tendency in criminology, or even of visual criminology proper, is not at all possible here. There are many moments of important visual scholarship in criminology that have no doubt escaped consideration here. Rather than an offer exhaustive list of examples of the visual criminological tendency, this book simply aims to briefly describe how, why, and from where a visual criminology emerged, and then to offer some examples of how it looks when we encounter it.

The book

If we are surrounded by images, and if the power of those images is ascendant, a criminological reckoning with them only makes sense. This book is an effort to both show how that *has been* done, and how that *might be* done. This introductory chapter, then, has already started us down that path and set the stage for the rest of the book by first describing the development of visual criminology from already-existing criminological tendencies and offering up some brief engagement with some of the key concepts that inform and condition my thinking on the subject.

Chapter 2, 'The Visual in Social Science', steps back from the distinctly criminological study of the visual with which the book is primarily concerned with a brief and truncated description of the ways in which visual criminology is informed by visual research, methods, and theory developed in other disciplinary arenas including sociology, anthropology, and visual and cultural theory. This chapter will also briefly introduce some key concepts that will inform the rest of the book.

In Chapter 3, 'Visual Methods in Criminology', we will move from the 'what?' to the 'how?' with a discussion and outline of the methodological trends and tendencies that have, so far, been favored, developed, or otherwise employed by visual criminologists. From photo-elicitation interviewing, to the production of original images as part of a research agenda, to the analysis of existing images, this chapter is intended to offer a glimpse across the horizon of the methodological practice and possibility of a visual criminology.

From there, the book turns towards four distinct sites and themes already familiar to criminology in order to attempt to demonstrate what a visual criminological analysis might look like, which categories have already been most robustly taken up by visual criminologists, and some potential future directions for visual study. These four chapters, which cover environmental harm, drugs, prisons and punishment, and, finally, police, represent what we might, for our purposes here, imagine as four of the central sites and themes of critical criminological inquiry and interest. These themes, as mentioned previously, are also broadly representative of some of the areas of interest that have most clearly generated, fostered, and employed the visual tendency in criminology.

In the first of these thematic chapters, Chapter 4, 'Environmental Harm and the Visual', I describe and consider some of the ways in which environmental harm and change are taken up by criminology, the role of the visual in constructing social perceptions of 'the environment' and environmental change, and the ways that visual criminology might continue to inform criminologies of environmental harm.

The green criminology of Chapter 4 has been, as described earlier, remarkably generative as a site of development for visual criminology, and the same can be said for critical criminologies of drugs, which have also contributed significantly to the visual criminological enterprise. Chapter 5, 'Drugs and the Visual', traces the outlines of drugs as they appear visually and criminologically, with a particular focus on the ways in which drug images influence and guide drug policy and criminal justice philosophy and action, and the ways in which drug images have contributed to global trends in mass incarceration and policing.

The essential criminological sites of punishment, prisons, and police emerge fully in the final two thematic chapters. In the first of these, Chapter 6, 'Punishment, Prisons, and the Visual', I consider the ways and sites in which punishment and the visual image intersect. Here, particular interest is given to the role of the image in constructing and communicating a carceral culture in which the figure of the penal apparatus always looms. This chapter also devotes significant attention to describing the material, cognitive, and cultural techniques and tendencies through which the prison either emerges into or recedes from view.

With the final thematic chapter, 'Police and the Visual' (Chapter 7), I turn my attention to issues of police, policing, and the role of the image and the visual in constructing, reifying, expressing, and resisting police power. Of particular interest in this chapter are the ways in which the ideology of police asserts itself into the visual, and the ways in which the image work of police is produced across visual fields. Like the carceral images that configure the entire visual culture from which they emerge, police images produce and naturalize a distinct police 'point of view' that conditions the social and political contexts from and into which it emerges. In each of these substantive chapters, I offer a number of examples of the images most relevant for criminology, and of the moments in which the criminological image comes to life most clearly. While I have made efforts to resist any particular regionalism, examples are nevertheless drawn primarily from an American context.

Finally, in the concluding chapter, the book ends with some thoughts on the blind spots that persist in visual criminology, but more generally in the very ways in which we conceptualize and act upon knowledge. In particular, this final chapter describes some of the problems with a visual criminology that reproduces the privileged position of sight and vision over other ways of knowing, other perceptual modalities that, like vision, can provide unique and singular insights into the social worlds of crime, harm, and justice.

2

The Visual in Social Science

Introduction

Visual criminology did not emerge solely from the critical and cultural criminologies described in the previous chapter. Rather, its development represents criminology adopting and adapting certain tendencies already at play in other areas. While its influences are as vast and diverse as its iterations—there are, it seems, as many visual epistemologies as there are visual criminologists—we can nevertheless locate and note them. This chapter begins by doing just that: by considering and describing the ways that scholarly attention is paid to the optical, mechanical, processual, political, and material forces that shape and condition the social world through the image. From there, I offer some loose and flexible definitions of some key concepts, as well as some efforts to operationalize some of those concepts so that their role in informing my own analysis can (hopefully and helpfully) be clear.

This is not, though, meant to be an account of these developments that is anywhere near comprehensive. For one, such an account would immediately exceed the remit and scope of this book. Moreover, though, the broad interdisciplinarity of 'visual studies' (a formation discussed thoroughly later in this chapter) in which we can more or less place the trends and developments discussed here almost necessarily leads to reiteration; while the refinements made by visual sociologists of course differ from those made by visual anthropologists, to describe each development exhaustively and to tease out the (important, but often minor) distinctions between orientations, thinkers, methods, and so on would be to lose sight of our topic—visual criminology—which, while growing up at the knee of these other disciplinary formations, has quickly come into its own.

Visual sociology

Of the various disciplinary antecedents of visual criminology, its most obvious roots are probably in visual sociology. From the earliest days of the discipline, sociology—and anthropology, too, discussed in the next section—both regularly utilized the visual, particularly in the routine administrative documentation of research. For sociologists, the photographic image was a way to illustrate and communicate some of the optically observable traits of subjects and sites of study, a practice that was closely tied to the spirit of social reform and progress that occupied early sociologists (Carrabine 2015: 105–6). Eventually, though, the production of photographic images as a dimension of social research fell from favor, as both sociology and anthropology began to view the relatively amateurish photographic efforts of researchers as subjectively and unsystematically producing uselessly mundane and unsophisticated images (see generally Pink 2020: 19).

The influence of visual thinking in sociology is, of course, not at all surprising, given that criminology writ large is itself a branch on the sociological family tree. From Michel Foucault to Howard Becker, the visual impulse in sociology is strong, preconfiguring the visual tendency in criminology. We might also note, briefly, that the same sociological impulse—an urge to uncover and fully see the dynamics of social relations that make our worlds—conditions a popular or public visual sociology, one evident in everything from the contemporary social impulse to document everyday life using cellphone cameras to the wild and enduring popularity of documentary cinema.

The development of visual sociology was inevitable, given that, as sociologist Douglas Harper notes, the disciplines of photography—what Harper calls a 'new way of seeing'[1]—and sociology—'a new lens of interpreting'—were born in Europe during the same decades and 'as products of the same social events' (Harper 1988: 55). In Harper's account of its development, early visual sociology was chiefly interested in the storytelling power of the photographic image, its evidentiary and documentary potential. Here, photo-makers working at the earliest moments of the form produced images that, Harper argues, could have easily and without any meaningful concern stood in for the descriptions of conditions among the English working class offered only a few decades earlier by Marx. Harper goes on to describe the role photographic sociology *could have* played in illustrating and enlivening the sorts of early 'community studies' that would prove foundational in American sociology. Unfortunately, as Harper (1988: 58) describes, 'sociology found little place for a visual approach' and so 'from the 1920s to the 1960s there was no visual sociology'. Harper argues that the dearth of visual sociology in this period is attributable to the focus on survey methods and other research methodologies that expressly sought to distance researchers from subjects (an impulse that, in my estimation, is mostly incompatible with the intimacy of human-subject photography) and the fact that the methods favored at and by the University of Chicago, where most of the significant methodological innovation was underway, did not include visual data.

And, really, in Harper's 1988 formulation, visual sociology more or less begins and ends with the 'taking' and 'analyzing' of optical images. Here, according to Harper, 'visual sociology is a collection of approaches in which researchers use photographs to portray, describe, or analyze social phenomena' (1988: 55) that can be comprehensively categorized into either *taking* photographs or *analyzing* photographs. No sociologist is more emblematic of this tendency and approach than Becker, whose long and storied sociological career has just about always included and accommodated his interest in photography, and Becker has contributed significantly to the development and description of the visual sociological tendency (see generally Becker 1979, 1995, 2002). For Becker, though—and, really, for the bulk of visual sociology— those are primarily methodological tendencies, rather than theoretical ones. In some sense, then, we might imagine that as in other areas of development, sociology did much of the early heavy lifting, and so by the time visual criminology emerged, it could do so with a more holistic interest than its sociological forebear.

While the assessment offered by Harper is a fitting description of the 'visual sociology' of the 1980s—and, indeed, would not seem like an erroneous description of early 'visual criminology', in the sense that both would not be visual so much as visible—it would come to be outmoded by a holistically visual sociology that, like visual criminology, is more attentive to the processual dimensions of the image and the ways in which images *do* and *mean* more than the sum of their parts. In this more comprehensive sociological accounting for the visual, according to Luc Pauwels, a visual tendency emerges that moves (a bit) beyond making and analyzing images, instead training its attention on the ways in which valuable sociological knowledge can be developed by 'observing, analyzing, and theorizing [society's] visual manifestations' (2015: 3).

Pauwels, whose framework for visual sociology nudges the field closer to a comprehensive interest in visual processes, like Rafter and other foundational thinkers in visual criminology, notes (perhaps obviously, but still compellingly) that communicating sociological knowledge through visual engagement is an approach with deep potential. While sociological work in this vein is perhaps more insistently methodological than the visual criminology of today, visual criminologists pursuing approaches like documentary criminology and the production of original images as part of a research agenda will surely find it a useful complement to some of the important methodological work already underway in those areas (Carrabine 2015; Natali 2016; Natali and McClanahan 2017, 2020; Redmon 2017, 2018).

Visual anthropology

Just as the visual tendency in criminology emerged from sociology, so too did it arise (in both sociology and criminology, in fact) from anthropology. For as long as the study of human groups and populations has existed, anthropologists have used representational images—photographs and films, but also illustrations, sculpture, and other forms of visual media—in order to aid in the description and categorization of human groups, behaviors, maladies, and so on. This tendency in anthropology, it is worth noting, stretches across both biological and social variants of the discipline; indeed, as with Lombroso and his 'criminal anthropology' (West 2017, 2019), biological anthropologists rely (not entirely, of course, but significantly) on the visual appearances of subjects of study, while sociocultural anthropologists use images, for example, in order to document and communicate sociocultural behaviors. It is the latter anthropological tendency—a more process-oriented and conceptual interest in 'the visual' —that most informs visual criminology by way of visual sociology, although it still more or less casts an interest in the image as an interest in the visual.

Even in most sociocultural visual anthropology, 'the visual' remains primarily a methodological tool, a site of analysis, rather than a conceptual field. As Marcus Banks and Howard Morphy (1999: 1) describe out the outset of their seminal (edited) collection of essays on visual anthropology, the field 'lies at the interfaces between anthropology and its audiences'. In this stream of anthropology, exemplified also in collections from John Collier Jr and Malcolm Collier (1967) to Paul Hockings (1999), the image functions first and foremost as a communicative device. Indeed, among the first and most influential calls for a visual anthropology, is Collier and Collier's *Visual Anthropology* (1967), subtitled *Photography as a Research Method*. Although not representative of the conceptual boundaries of the field, this variation of visual anthropology has certainly influenced visual criminology as it exists today—particularly evident in the serious and thoughtful use of visual methods such as those developed in and by documentary criminology (Hayward 2017; Redmon 2017, 2018).

Visual studies and visual theory

Although the disciplinary strands of visual sociology and visual anthropology have all contributed hugely to the emergence and development of the visual tendency in criminology and, ultimately, visual criminology proper, it has largely emerged not from one antecedent tradition, but rather from what we can think of as simply 'visual studies'. In this context, we can imagine visual studies as emerging from the 'visual turn' of the 1980s and 1990s represented by the developments in visual sociology and anthropology described earlier, but also by a broader shift across disciplinary boundaries towards an interest in the visual and visible, and to reading the image as textually legitimate.[2]

As W.J.T. Mitchell describes it, visual studies is a precarious discipline, if it even makes sense to think of it in disciplinary terms. For Mitchell—a prominent figure in the critique of visual cultures—the field is 'quite unnecessary' owing largely to its 'ambiguous relation to art history and aesthetics' as disciplinary siblings (2005: 339). That same ambiguity, though, has resulted in a broad tendency under which authors and ideas have emerged in order to make both sense and nonsense of the image and the visual, and visual criminology has reaped the rewards in the form of a vast and diverse literature from which to draw.

The strengths of visual studies, we might imagine, are much the same as the strengths that have made cultural criminology so central in the development of visual criminology. Similar to the sort of theoretical and methodological promiscuity that characterizes cultural criminology, visual studies is constituted by contributions from sociology, anthropology, geography, literary theory, critical theory, art history, aesthetics, American studies, and a host of other disciplines, subdisciplines, and sub-subdisciplines. Most notably, perhaps, visual studies shares its DNA with cultural studies and, relatedly, critical cultural and social theory. Visual studies, we might assume because of the very breadth described here, represents a host of approaches to thinking about and researching visual culture (the general object of its study), including methodological insights, theoretical concerns, and critical political and polemical work on the image and the visual, and it is in this constellation of thought that some of the most generative and enduring debates and insights surrounding visual culture have emerged. As a distinct field of study, visual studies is also, like visual criminology, somewhat inherently critical: like the critical and cultural criminologies that gave rise to visual criminology, work on visual cultures is deeply influenced by developments in cultural studies, particularly the foundational work of Stuart Hall (see Hall et al [1978] for the most enduring of Hall's contributions to critical criminology), whose insistence on maintaining fidelity to a critical Marxist analysis and simultaneous rejection of disciplinary dogma is surely familiar to critical and cultural criminologies (Hall 1992).

Important work to emerge from visual studies includes that by Ariella Azoulay, who imagines photography as an intensely active process in her considerations of the role of optical image making in the construction of political subjectivities and civil society (2008; 2015). Jacques Rancière (2009: 8), too, whose work on aesthetics (discussed later in this section) has been foundational in visual studies, notes 'the long struggle of photographers to affirm that photography was not merely mechanical reproduction', calling our attention not only to an essential point since adopted by visual criminology, but also to the contributions to visual theory made by Walter Benjamin, Theodore Adorno and other critical theorists of the Frankfurt School, where the image and visual culture were approached with great care and philosophical interest. Critical insights from that tradition include Benjamin's concern, as indicated in his titular focus on mechanical reproduction, with the challenges posed by photography and by an increasingly industrially and mechanically mediated lived experience to cultural and artistic value, as well as to human ontology and subjectivity (Benjamin 2008).

In thinking expressly about photography, Rancière and Azoulay join others who have contributed to the broad paradigms of visual studies, including photographer, theorist, and critic Alan Sekula, whose work on the ways in which the history of photography implicates state violence and power and, at its inception, the new technology—understood at the time, according to Sekula, as 'modernity run riot' — 'threatened to overrun the citadels of high culture' while at once 'promis[ing] an enhanced mastery of nature' (Sekula 1986: 4–5). John Tagg, too, dedicates his thinking largely to the development of photography not only as a mechanical capacity, but also as a political technology essential in the historical development of political economy, contemporary subjectivity, and state power (see generally Tagg 1982, 1993). The echoes of this work, it seems to me, plainly reverberate across a contemporary visual criminology that is, first and foremost, concerned with the role of images and the visual in constructing, reifying, naturalizing, resisting, reproducing, and communicating power.

Like the visual in visual criminology, though, the visual in visual studies is not all about the photographic image. Instead, it points to a broad concern with the entire expanse of visual culture, to include cinema, painting, and everyday images. Cinema, perhaps unsurprisingly, has attracted serious and sustained attention. Just as others have developed our understanding of the photographic mode of production, Jonathan Beller (2012) has outlined the ways in which the 'cinematic mode of production' suggests that visual cultures are 'deterratorialized factories in which spectators work' at the production of value (2012: 250). Gilles Deleuze, meanwhile, provides a dense but comprehensive example of how cinematographic images are animated by—and animate—philosophy. Tracing the shift in cinema, after the Second World War, from what he calls 'the movement image' that characterized pre-war cinema to the 'time image' that characterizes post-war cinema, Deleuze explores the signs and semiotics of the cinematic in order to develop a taxonomy of the visual image. In both volumes of his central work on cinema, Deleuze maintains an analytical interest in the constituent parts of the form including frame, shot, and montage, insisting throughout that cinema is constituted by the relation of perception, affect, and action (Deleuze 1986, 2013). While we might not find Deleuze routinely appearing in the bibliographies of criminologists (although we probably should), we can nevertheless find ample evidence of the influence of his work on the moving image in some examples of visually attuned criminology (see generally McClanahan et al 2017; Linnemann and Turner 2020; McClanahan 2019). Deleuze's work on the relation between the temporal field and the cinematic image also suggests another important dimension of the visual (and visual criminology): the relationship between seeing, the visual, images, and temporality. Images, of course, help to fix us in history, and we rely quite significantly on sight and vision to mark time and its passage. We also use the development of the human capacity to mechanically capture images to mark and delineate time in an epochal sense, as we divide human history into discreet eras and moments marked by their relation to photography, cinema, and visual art.

Finally, a number of contributions to the broad field of visual studies have come from the field of aesthetics. Referring generally to the ways in which our senses guide us through the world, albeit with an outsized focus on the visual (discussed later, in the final chapter of this book), aesthetics as an object and site of critical inquiry is closely tied to the critical social, cultural, and political theory of the Frankfurt School, where the various developments in Western art were read for the ways in which they both reflected the political tendencies of the day and presaged coming critical cultural and political formations, and in the work of Rancière, who in in what are widely considered to be two of critical theory and philosophy's greatest contemporary contributions to the study of aesthetics, *Dissensus* (2015) and *Aesthesis* (2013), describes the ways in which politics forms the base of aesthetics, and aesthetics in turn expresses and reifies politics. The questions on the sensory appearances of materiality raised in the study of aesthetics have also contributed to visual criminological tendencies, with Andrew Millie (2017, 2019) offering a proposal for an aesthetic criminology that shares significant DNA with the visual criminology outlined here. As Cynthia Freeland (2012: 399) has described, though, the field of aesthetics is 'consistently focused on "higher arts" such as painting, sculpture, and music'. While Millie demonstrates, then, the need for an 'aesthetic criminology', it is nevertheless important to suggest that both an aesthetic and a visual criminology work to avoid the high–low cultural binaries and 'visuocentrism' (Freeland 2012: 399; discussed more thoroughly in the final chapter of this book) of traditional studies of aesthetics.

Issues and concepts in visual social science

Although visual criminology remains a relatively open field without a lot of dogmatic constraints and concepts, it has nevertheless developed its own vocabulary, to some extent, and its concerns are nevertheless somewhat consistent. Many of these issues and concepts come to visual criminology by way of the sorts of visual formations in other social sciences described previously. It might be helpful, then, to offer up here some helpful points of guidance by loosely defining and describing some of the key terms and concepts that inform my analysis throughout the book.

This section also briefly presents some of the issues and problems that have arisen in and around visual social sciences. Just as visual criminology is somewhat lucky, having arrived late to the party, in that much of the heavy lifting of methodology has already been done, so too are we lucky that visual studies (to include, as described earlier, the full range of critical scholarly engagement with the dynamics of visual culture) has already begun to tackle critical issues and respond to critical questions and concerns.

Of all the issues in which the dynamics of the visual are most deeply and troublingly at work, perhaps none has the immediacy and critical materiality—at least in terms of crime and justice—of race. Race is, after all, an intensely visual category—our conception of race as a deduction of science, as mentioned in the previous chapter, has been conditioned significantly by the visual race science of Lombroso and other positivist (and, of course, racist) biosocial scientists—and, moreover, one that obviously co-implicates power, and so it is no surprise that academic inquiry into the overlapping dynamics of the visual, race, and power would be among the first to emerge from the visual turn. Here, visual anthropology is deeply implicated, largely because of the ways in which photography developed alongside anthropological practice, and the eagerness with which early and, in particular, colonial anthropologists adopted the practice of field photography. Of course, it is also worth mentioning that the construction of a racialized other through the visual predates photography, and so we can imagine that as long as we have looked and produced a representation, we have configured racial others through the image (S.M. Smith 2004, 2013). This process is also implicated clearly in contemporary culture, as it is entirely central to the ways in which violence and justice are distributed globally: from wars to drug laws, our racialized others come to us visually.

Sticking briefly with photography, we should also consider the ways in which race is implicated in the material practice of photography. In North America and Europe, as consumer photographic technologies become more widely available, photo-developing labs and technologies—including new consumer-grade color filmstock—started to quickly emerge to meet the demands of the new consumer market. Film developers and designers, though, struggled with creating a baseline standard by which to gauge 'corrections' to the color balance of an image, or even to guide the development of a type of film. In response to the problem, the industry developed what were called 'Shirley cards', tightly color-balanced images by which standards could be measured. The Shirley cards, though, categorically contained only images of white women, thereby making, through an alarmingly technocratic bit of racism, to make white women's skin the 'ideal standard for most North American analogue photo labs since the early part of the twentieth century' (Roth 2009: 112). As Sarah Lewis (2019) describes, film standards and the associated Shirley cards were eventually addressed, not in response to the concerns over the racial dimensions of film standards, but because companies that produced chocolate and wooden furniture began to complain of difficulties in accurately capturing the various tones of their products. These standards, Lorna Roth notes, continue to dominate today, and we see similar problems at the intersections of mechanical image capture and race in the more contemporary concerns over digital imaging technologies that often reproduce the same standards established in the early days of the commercial film industry. Relatedly, the visual technology of the archive can often reproduce the same material segregating and racist effects that condition the production of the image; as Eric Margolis (1999: 7) describes, '[archival] collections made under conditions of racial segregation are themselves segregated and continue to reproduce images of hierarchy and dominance'.

Frantz Fanon, in *The Fact of Blackness* (2016 [1952]), wrote of the ways in which racial Blackness and the Black self are constituted visually and relationally, and how Black life is structured by white vision in such a way that the ability and right to see the processes of history are managed and administrated, a condition of the power of visuality (described presently). Fred Moten (2008), meanwhile, picks up where Fanon left off, connecting Blackness (for Moten, interestingly enough, 'black' also takes on a purely chromatic character next to its human and sociocultural counterparts of 'Blacks' and 'Blackness') to a critical ontology and mode of being. Moten also, though, quite clearly draws a line connecting the conditions of (racial) Blackness and fugitivity, a point also taken up readily by visual criminology. Simone Browne (2015: 11) further underscores the ways in which racialized power relations are conditioned and configured by the visual, describing not only the centrality of racial and conceptual Blackness to the ways in which 'race [continues to] structure surveillance practice' but also the long history of the visual surveillance of Black people, communities, and movements.

The racialized visualities described by Fanon, Moten, Browne, and others, though, are not limited to the sort of racialized culture that we might assume to exist largely outside of the enlightened confines of academia. Rather, the same scholarly gazes that encourage and constitute the visual tendency in social sciences can themselves be understood as reflecting a distinctly racialized and white power to see and right to look. Returning to Fanon, who described the power of the 'colonial gaze' as central in the production of a criminalizable other, we can also find a plain link between visual frameworks of race science and the entangled dynamics of crime, harm, and justice. Similarly, social scientists have offered robust critiques of the ways in which sociological thought, conceptualized broadly, is configured through a distinctly white—and often colonial—way of seeing (see generally Ladner 1998; Saleh-Hanna 2017). In a contemporary mediated world in which Blackness continues to be a sort of visual shorthand for criminality and violence, and in which more and more racialized images of crime and justice are produced and disseminated every minute, the visual dimensions of race are sure to continue to compel a visual criminology.

Like race, gender has not only emerged as a chief concern in and for visual studies broadly, but has also appeared with some consistency as a concern for visual criminologists. Like race, too, the bulk of work in visual studies on issues of gender focuses on the role of the visual in constructing, patrolling, and policing the boundaries of gender (and, reflecting the sort of patriarchal power that most critical criminologists would take as a given, that increasingly means reproducing binary gender identity and expression). Finally, both race and gender are visually constituted and communicated and controlled, increasingly, in the online worlds of digital visual culture, an environment that Lisa Nakamura (2008) notes is particularly important in the constitution of racial and gender identities and formations because of its air of interactivity and exchange, in which gender and racial formation can be more fully explored.

The 'white gaze' described earlier, of course, is not just white; it is also male (Mulvey 1989). The images produced in and by dominant visual culture generally assume a male audience, and the processes of seeing are structured by the same white and heteronormative patriarchal power that structures Western capitalist social practice. Just as with race, gendered images and ways of seeing also play a significant role in the ways in which gender is produced, communicated, and policed (Knauss and Pezzoli-Olgiati 2015). Criminological images have played a particularly noteworthy role in these processes, too; Lombroso, in his enterprise of criminological positivist anthropology, made a study of what he believed to be physical expressions of criminality and atavism, and early and significant 'family studies' in criminology—which were largely based on the visual criminal anthropology of earlier positivists like Lombroso—such as Richard Dugdale's (1877) famed study of New York state's Jukes family made a particular point of focusing on women's criminal offending (for a fascinating historical description and analysis of that particular early stream of visual thinking in criminology, see Rafter 1988). The role of the criminological image in maintaining gender norms and relations is also, of course, still quite strong in contemporary settings. As is the case with race, media constructs gendered images of crime that support dominant hegemonic perspectives and narratives on social difference and power (Cavender et al 1999), and women are often cast into immediately deviant sexual roles, or into the role of helpless and hapless victim, using the logics of dominant gender formations (Jewkes and Linnemann 2017: 124). Gendered criminological images also, as May-Len Skilbrei (2013: 137) notes, play an important role in structuring mediated portrayals of gendered crime.

Images of suffering

Although it is well outside of the remit of this book to comprehensively describe the various and deeply significant ethical issues at work in visual criminology and other visual social sciences, those problems and concerns are plentiful enough that they do require some attention. Among the many issues presented by efforts to understand, represent, describe, or explain the social and processual (and, of course, political) power of the image, perhaps none are more critical than the always-intertwined problems of empathy and exploitation already implicated in the previous discussion on race and gender. In particular, a visual social science—be it criminology, sociology, anthropology, or any other—grounded in the production of original images will always be plagued by questions of methodological ethics, and it is easy to anticipate that those problems will be especially pronounced when dealing with precarious and often marginalized people.

For Phillipe Bourgois and Jeff Schonberg, whose *Righteous Dopefiend* (2009)—which documents the lives of injection drug users in San Francisco, California, and which is exemplary in its attention to the processes, practices, and forces at play in the production, intake, and analysis of images—stands as something like a gold standard for a photo-informed ethnography in contemporary visual social sciences, photographic documentation of 'those who live under extreme duress and distress' raises critical questions of exploitation and voyeurism. Moreover, for Bourgois and Schonberg, those questions are intensified by a critical public visual anthropology—quite similar, in its aims and origins, to Rafter's formulation of a public visual criminology that accounts for the ways that popular perceptions shape policy—that must be attentive to what Pierre Bourdieu (1990) called 'symbolic violence' and the ways that violence and structural inequality might be contained, produced, and reproduced in and by images of suffering.[3]

The considerable suffering captured by Bourgois and Schonberg, though—and, relatedly, similar photographic and ethnographic projects surrounding drugs, some of which are discussed more thoroughly in Chapter 5—is not the only sort of suffering that raises important issues of ethics and exploitation for visual social sciences. We might also consider forces of violence like war and armed conflict, which often are sites of production of images that have significant social power and that, just as often, implicate suffering and the same risks of voyeurism that trouble Bourgois and Schonberg. These sorts of images—such as the iconic 1968 photograph of the execution of Nguyễn Văn Lém, a captured fighter in the Viet Cong who was publicly and summarily

executed by Nguyễn Ngọc Loan, a general in the South Vietnamese
Army and chief of the Vietnamese National Police Force, who fired
a single shot at point blank range into Văn Lém in front of an NBC
camera crew and an Associated Press photographer, Eddie Adams—
have huge impacts on the social perceptions of violence and organized
conflict. Adams' image, for instance, went on to win the 1969 Pulitzer
Prize for news photography, and it is credited alongside other iconic
images of human suffering—most notably images of Vietnamese
children fleeing a village following an American napalm attack captured
in 1972 by another AP photojournalist, Nick Ut, which sit alongside
Adams image as among the most iconic photographs ever taken—
with galvanizing public resistance to the conflict. These 'spectacles of
suffering', as Carrabine (2012: 466) puts it,[4] 'can transform the way
we live with, and understand, one another'.

There are also, of course, serious limitations and constraints on
the power of the spectacle of suffering to have such emancipatory
outcomes. Nearly every serious effort to think about the power of the
visual will, at one point or another, turn to questions of the tension
between action and numbness in the face of such images of suffering
and atrocity, what Susan Sontag (1977: 15) called the power of the
image of atrocity and human suffering to both 'transfix' and 'anesthetize'
its audience, to either suggest or to foreclose entirely on the possibility
of action. As Sontag describes it, although 'an event known through
photographs certainly becomes more real than it would have been if
one had never seen the photographs', 'the shock of photographed
atrocities wears off with repeated viewings'. Although Sontag would
later return to the questions raised by images of suffering and atrocity
(specifically, here, in images of war and torture), ultimately concluding
that, despite the ways in which 'shock can become familiar' and the
intended or de facto audience of an image can simply 'not look' as part
of a 'means to defend themselves against what is upsetting', images of
atrocity, suffering, and harm have a social power 'that does not abate'.

Central to Sontag's thinking on the ethical capacities of the visual
and of the image—particularly the photographic image, and more
particularly the photographic image as associated with human suffering
in war—are questions of grievability (and, relatedly, the notion of
'valid life') and its relation to the image. Taken up most notably by
Judith Butler (2006, 2016), questions of grievability surround the ways
in which suffering is understood and the response its understanding
engenders, and those processes are enacted, perhaps most significantly,
in and through the image. For Butler, grievability is affirmed or negated
in the image of wartime suffering, a space in which the materiality

of conflict is reflected and reified in the materiality of the image. Butler, in her analysis of the photographs of torture taken in 2003 at the American-run Abu Ghraib prison in Iraq and later leaked to international media, also returns us to the question of racialization and the construction of the racialized other, noting that, in the process of framing images of the torture at Abu Ghraib and the broader American occupation of Iraq, the figure of a primitive and backwards Muslim other emerged that explained and justified those same images of war and torture. Central to Butler's analysis is a conceptual scaffolding of frames and framing, the processes by which images are taken in and made sense of and, according to Butler, which 'delimits the visual field itself', are questions that quite plainly speak to the sorts of concerns that condition not only visual criminology, but also all other critical areas of visual studies. Questions of valid life and grievability, for example, plainly configure our perceptions of images of suffering prisoners and victims of police violence, drug users and those involved in illegal economies, and even environmental harm (see generally Turner 2019). Also taking up the torture at Abu Ghraib—or, more accurately, the social reaction to images of the torture—Carrabine describes the expectation that we will empathically register the suffering and 'misery of distant strangers' as a recent development, noting that mediated spectacles of suffering have always had 'considerable social complexity' (2011: 19). It might also be instructive to approach the images of torture at Abu Ghraib—and, for that matter, other images of the sorts of atrocity we are generally aware of but that nevertheless remains mostly unseen, such as the prison or the animal agriculture industry (McClanahan and Linnemann 2018)—from a perspective informed by Roland Barthes (1972: 151), whose idea of inoculation describes the ways in which the exposure of shocking images like those from Abu Ghraib 'immunizes the contents of the collective imagination by means of a small inoculation of acknowledged evil' in order to hide a greater and more essential atrocity. Sociologist and criminologist Stan Cohen (2013: 16) described a similar process, in the context of the torture of Palestinian criminal suspects at the hands of Israeli police interrogators, by which 'something whose existence could [previously] not be admitted' comes to be seen through inoculating images and discourses as 'predictable'.

It is also worth noting here that in his work on the various ethical issues that haunt visual social science, Carrabine (2012) describes a tension between the ways that the photographs of Diane Arbus were received and understood by Sontag, who found Arbus' images of 'freaks' and outcasts to be horrifyingly exploitative, flattening, and cruel, and how those same images were received and read by Cohen as entirely different, notable for their complexity and liberatory potential. As Carrabine describes, the tension between these two ways of seeing between 'two people inhabiting the same moral world' perfectly illustrates the ways in which we can 'see the same images in radically different ways' (Cohen 2013: 299, quoted in Carrabine 2012: 477).

The *form* of an image, too, does some work in dictating or determining its reception, and so the mode of original images also have implications for ethical decision making in visual criminological research. Portraiture, for example—what we can summarize for our purposes here as non-candid or posed images of a human subject that retain a focus on the subject's face and its features—presents distinct issues of power, and portraits have long been important visual objects through which we construct knowledge and gravitas. But while portrait photography can certainly arouse compassion, an effect that is a central (if idealized) aim of most photographic portraiture (Johnson 2011), it can also arouse derision. Photographic portrait making, of course, supplanted earlier and wildly popular painted portraiture in one of the most immediate adoptions of new photographic technologies. For artist, writer, and critic John Berger (2016), the death of the painted portrait is nothing to lament, largely because of how fully its utility was diminished by the advent of photography, which promised a more informationally rich portraiture. Still, though, for the subject, a photographic portrait may 'read' as a true, honest image of self, or, conversely, a portrait may 'read' as a distorted visual image, or as an essentializing and flattening reproduction of self. Portraits also, from a subject's perspective, are a bit like being alienated from the (affective and emotional) labor of being, and so it is easy to imagine the ways in which the distinct mode of the portrait presents issues for an ethically sound visual criminological method, and so the careful contextualization of images becomes paramount (Copes et al 2019).

Ultimately, the ethical dimensions and concerns of visual criminology are largely shared across other fields of visual research. Those issues, of course, are likely to be most pronounced when dealing with methodologies and methods that encourage or require the production of original images, particularly those with human subjects, and almost always implicate the entangled issues of exploitation and suffering (or, more precisely, exploitation of suffering). While there is no ethical handbook, and while a full accounting of the ethical dimensions of the visual and the image is wildly outside of the scope of this book, there are thankfully ample contributions (see generally Kleinman and Kleinman 1996; Gross et al 2003; Valier and Lippens 2004; Boxall and

Ralph 2009; for a distinctly criminological description of these issues, see Carrabine 2012) from across social sciences that can inform and guide visual criminology as it continues to develop in ways that require methodological sensitivity and thoughtfulness.

Images, evidence, and knowing

Among the central concerns of a visually attuned study of the dynamics of harm, crime, and justice—whether it comes from criminology, sociology, visual studies, or any other discipline—are questions surrounding the evidentiary potential and dimension of the image and, relatedly, of the role of the visual and seeing in constructing knowledge. Among the 'natural worlds' over which early photography promised an enhanced human mastery is, of course, the world of objective truth. The image as evidence,[5] though, is every bit as contested as every other image, and the processes that produce valid evidentiary images are the same as the processes that produce, frame, and condition all other images.

Criminologist Katherine Biber carries on Alison Young's earlier interest in the ways that images act in and on law, describing the ways in which the dynamics of visibility and invisibility emerge in the process of redaction, in which the construction of truth and knowledge becomes an administrative practice. For Biber, whose core interest is in the ways in which the archives of images produced by administrative and bureaucratic practice constitute (and converse with) artistic practice and objects (Biber and Dalton 2009; Biber 2013, 2018; Biber and Luker 2014), the redaction practice is also an expression of a bureaucratic and administrative artistic practice, a perspective that highlights the role of legal power and politics in constructing contemporary knowledge. The redacted documents considered by Biber (and, also relatedly, by visual artist and critic Jenny Holzer in her *Redaction* series of paintings and prints, which is a fine example of an unavoidably political visual artistic practice) are, interestingly, exemplary of the ways in which the textual and the visual bleed into and overlap with one another, the boundaries between them growing fuzzier every day as our world becomes mediated more and more by visual–textual hybrids, and the ways in which they nevertheless steadfastly determine truth and constitute knowledge. Moreover, because evidentiary images almost necessarily implicate historical discontinuity—they nearly always imply change, an issue described more thoroughly in Chapter 4—their role in the construction of history is always there, too, in ways that suggest and affirm the construction of truth, history, knowledge, and power through the processes of visuality.

The evidentiary dimensions of the visual image, though, are also complicated by other factors, and so again are every bit as contested and contestable as any other image or visual field. One of these complicating factors is that images are capable of doing more than one type of work: just as images reveal, they can also conceal, and the unseen world is of course far greater than the seen one (Smith 2013). This simple but seemingly contradictory condition and tension between seen and unseen is at the heart of critical visual studies—including visual criminology—and emerges in theory, as with questions about the ways in which sites of power might be concealed or obscured (Glazek 2012; Linnemann and Medley 2019; McClanahan and Linnemann 2018) and in methods (see generally Armstrong 2010).

Another complicating factor of the image as evidence is the contested terrain of realism. While photography and the photographic image have, since their inception, been understood as technologies of the real—photography, after all, constituted 'a new juridical photographic realism' (Sekula 1986: 5) upon the court's recognition of its evidentiary potential—a critical approach to analyzing the forces of visual culture should strive to constantly unsettle and renegotiate that understanding. If we accept the postmodern explanation of our cultural conditions, anyway, realism loses most of its salience, and visual realism is doubly challenged by the growing prevalence and sophistication of post-real imaging technologies and techniques like 'deep fakes', described here in the final chapter. Similarly, we might imagine the capitalist realism described in Mark Fisher's (2009) framework as deeply visual, by way of its focus on imaginative processes of capitalist subjectivity, and that the power and ubiquity of his capitalist realism negates the potential of a contemporary visual realism free from the influence of capital.

Finally, any visually attuned exploration of social relations must be mindful of the ways in which evidence and knowing are not as perfectly intertwined as we might hope or imagine. As Cohen described, the power to reject or disavow evidence extends to even the most powerful and seemingly irrefutable knowledges. For Cohen, this is part of a complex sociological process of strategic denial, and it is framed throughout his work, in part, as a technique by which we manage our individual and cultural relationships with the visual, the image, knowledge, and suffering. Sociologist Linsey McGoey (2012: 553) calls the ignorance produced by strategic denial of evidence and knowledge a 'productive asset, helping individuals and institutions to command resources, deny liability in the aftermath of crises, and to assert expertise'. Applied to the ways and degree to which we are routinely exposed to criminological images of suffering—which, of course, permeate nearly every corner of mediated contemporary visual culture—it certainly seems that the production of ignorance is an essential technique in the management of our knowledge of the everyday suffering brought to bear by processes of criminal justice.

Visuality and countervisuality

A central pillar among the many frameworks that have contributed to the development of visual criminology, and also to my own thinking on the interplay between images, crime, harm, and justice, is Nicholas Mirzoeff's theoretical framework of 'visuality'. Influential, across various disciplines, in the ways in which the social and relational power of the visual is understood, Mirzoeff's conceptualization of visuality draws together the right to look and act of seeing, the image, power, and history. In this framework, visuality as a power 'visualizes history to sustain autocratic authority' (2011b: 475) and enjoys a power to define and classify and naturalize, 'sutur[ing] authority to power and render[ing] the association natural' (2011a: 6). For Mirzoeff, visuality is a relational power, 'the authority to tell us to move on, that exclusive claim to the right to look' (2011b: 474). Perhaps most importantly, though, Mirzoeff's visuality expressly 'is not a trendy theory word meaning the totality of all visual images and devices' (2011b: 474). Rather, as he clarifies, it is a perceptual process, one in which power is manifested and acted through. Visuality is the power that restrains or grants the right to look.

Mirzoeff's theory of visuality also accounts for visuality's antipode, the countervisual. Like visuality, of course, countervisuality is more than the totality of all critical images and devices, or all images and devices that run counter to power. Instead, like its opposition, countervisuality is relational and processual, 'combining information, imagination, and insight' (2011a: 3). While Mirzoeff's visuality has been influential in the development of visual criminology, it is through the particular lens of the countervisual that most of that work has gazed (see generally Schept 2014; Brown 2017). Some of this tendency, we might assume, is an artefact of visual criminology's close ties to streams of critical and cultural criminology that are often uniquely interested in cultural dissent, art and activism, social movements, and a broadly conceptualized 'resistance', each of which are often distinctly visual. It is also, though, likely an outcome of criminology's interest—sometimes overt, sometimes not—in power: the 'naturalization' that is at the heart of visuality ultimately obscures power, and it becomes far more possible to reveal power relations in the 'realism' (Mirzoeff 2011a, 2011b: 5) of the countervisual.

Just as it is essential to keep in mind that 'visuality' is not just the totality of all images or all visual culture(s), it is equally important to note that countervisuality is not just some contrarian version of that same reduction: it is not just a parallel body of images that push against hegemonic visuality. In order to understand those images and visions that are clearly apart from hegemonic visuality, a useful distinction might be drawn between counter-images and countervisuality: a countervisual tendency or impulse might produce counter-images, but that production does not necessarily imply a fully formed countervisual vantage point. Among the powers of visuality, is the power to co-opt, recast, redact, or absorb the counter-image, and so there are always limits to the political or analytical utility of the counter-image.

Spectacle

Finally, a central theme and influence in visual thinking in social science in general—and, in particular, in visual criminology (again, likely, because of the early influence of cultural criminology)—is French social theorist and Situationist Guy Debord's (2012) concept of 'spectacle'. For Debord, 'modern conditions of production' result in the 'immense accumulation of spectacles' with all things 'directly lived' reduced 'into a representation' that constitutes the 'present model of … life'. While Debord's thinking on spectacle has deep implications for the notion that the representational image is fixed in its relation to truth—he insists, for example, that 'the true is a moment of the false'—his most useful aphorisms are far more inextricably tied to the central analytical conceit of the visual criminology outlined here: 'the spectacle is not a collection of images, but a social relation among people, mediated by images' (Debord 2012) (the spectacle, in this sense, is similar to Mirzoeff's visuality). If we were to make one slight tweak, we might replace 'images' here with 'the visual', in order to more fully get at the breathtaking scope of the forms and modes taken by the image, and in order to more fully implicate the processes of seeing in mediating social relations. Debord also notes that power—'the oldest specialization'—is 'at the root of the spectacle', and that 'the spectacle is capital accumulated', both points that further suggest the centrality of power to the image, the visual, and visuality; while Mirzoeff reflects something like a diffuse Foucauldian read of the relation between the visual and power, Debord locates power much more directly—and perhaps crudely, though certainly not unsatisfyingly—in capital.

Conclusion

This chapter has briefly sketched an outline of the trends and tendencies and streams of thought in the social sciences that have conditioned the formation of the visual criminology described in this book. While some of the earliest developments in visual social science were purely concerned with the methodologically sound production of original images, such material concerns are balanced and complemented by more conceptual ones in which 'the visual' comes alive outside of 'the image'.

Visual social sciences have also laid the groundwork for a visual criminology that is not only sensitive to the potential pitfalls in image making as part of a research agenda, but that is also sensitive and attentive to the ways that the visual has constructed social difference along the lines of race, class, and gender. When we think of visuality as a historical power, one that constitutes the right to look, we can see the myriad ways in which that power acts on social relation to affirm and offer an architecture of logic and naturalization to harm and oppression.

Visual criminology, as described here, is built on foundations that are both robust and critical. Although to account for the full scope of its influences would be impossible here, this chapter has described the pathways of visual thinking about the world that have led us to this point, where we find a new robust and critical orientation before us. The questions for the rest of this book, then, more generally concern the 'how?' questions of visual criminology: how is visual criminology produced, and how might it look when we encounter it? In the next chapter, I turn to the first of those questions by describing some of the methodological strategies and tendencies favored by visual criminology.

Visual Methods in Criminology

Introduction

Like any other sort of material entering the context of criminological analysis, the visual can be approached, managed, decoded, produced, and considered in any number of ways. This chapter describes some of those ways, and notes instances in which a number of visual methods are already evident within criminology. We should keep in mind, though, that visual methodologies—like other qualitative methodologies—are often so peculiar and particular that they are developed individually, in order that they best suit the context of their use. Moreover, we should remember that despite their occasional fuzziness, methods and methodologies are actual things, and that sometimes—or, really, most of the time—what we call visual criminology is less concerned with and conditioned by method than it is by something more like tendency. Rather than rigorously outline the boundaries of visual criminological methods, I think it is essential that visual criminology instead perhaps borrow the sort of (anti)methodological promiscuity that already configures and informs cultural criminology (see generally Ferrell 2009; Hayward and Presdee 2010). A truly comprehensive overview, then, is a challenge that is impossible to meet in a short chapter (or even a short book). Rather than endeavor to offer such an overview, I simply describe the most common—and, I think, the most fruitful and promising—avenues of visual research already opened by and within criminology.

There are, it goes almost without saying, any number of ways in which criminology might methodologically approach the visual. The first task, it seems to me, is to parse the various approaches and tendencies along the first obvious point of cleavage: the origin of the image under the scrutiny of analysis. In what follows, I start by drawing a line separating a visual criminological method that trains its gaze on existing images and one that orients itself towards the production of original images. Finally, I turn my attention to what we might think of, perhaps, as a third broad methodological orientation for visual criminology: a method that is not so concerned with the provenance of the image, but rather with the ways in which images might be deployed as a part of methodological agendas in order to lead to or draw out new paths of insight into the social and material worlds of crime and harm.

First, though, let us briefly consider the ways in which the various methods discussed here have themselves developed, and the ways in which that development has conditioned contemporary images of 'visual' research.

Producing original criminological images

Among the various ways in which the visual image has been employed across the social sciences, perhaps the most foundational is the sort of production of original images favored by visual sociologies and anthropologies described in the previous chapter. This tendency's prominence in criminology is, in large part, due to the prominence of photographic picture making as part of anthropological research agendas; for decades, the image of the anthropologist has been dominated by the vision of the curious and pith-helmeted Western bushwhacker, pad and pen in one hand, camera in the other. As outdated as that image may be, the production of original images in the field—or just in the processes—of research does, of course, have much to offer to the criminological enterprise. In the following sections, I describe two different ways in which the production of original images might serve a visual criminological agenda. The first, which is discussed only briefly, concerns the power of the camera to transform ways of seeing. The second, which seems to me to be far more significant for a visual criminology, concerns the image as evidence of harm.

We can start with the general assumption that most field-based research, in criminology or otherwise, involves a camera. This seems almost inevitably true in a world so occupied with documentation and representation, and doubly so in a world in which we all, more or less, have a camera in our pocket at all times. Much has been written elsewhere about the power of those ubiquitous lenses to change the way we see. Looking through the lens of a camera, the logic goes, presents a different picture than looking with the eyes alone. Similarly, of course, looking at a picture of a thing or a scene or a person is different from looking directly at the same thing or scene or person. As I have argued in other venues (McClanahan 2017; Natali and McClanahan 2020), though, there is a certain methodological or analytical power that comes from the act of looking through the mediating lens, of centering the criminological gaze in the mechanical frame. By simply moving through the research environment with a lens and the intent to make images, one becomes attuned to the dynamics of visibility, framing, composition, light, and shadow that produce the photographic image. In turn, a visually attuned criminologist may find themselves welcoming new insights into the affective dimensions of power and subjectivity, or the ways in which social phenomena might fade in and out of focus. Alternatively, images produced in the field might serve a far less ambitious—although no less important—purpose as evidentiary objects that function to establish the presence of crime, harm, or other phenomena.

If the old maxim is true—if seeing really is believing—then the evidentiary power of the image is already immediately clear. Deploying the full evidentiary power of the visual is, it seems, particularly useful for a critical visual criminology that follows other critical criminological paths by training its gaze on harm rather than crime. While the picture-making techniques and methodologies of early visual anthropologists—and, indeed, almost all anthropology, explicitly visual or otherwise—served primarily to assert and establish a spatial–temporal relation between the researcher and their subject-field ('I was here, and here is the proof'), criminologists might produce images to prove or assert moments of harm. Images here might be constructed and composed to communicate harm to an individual, group, and so forth. This sort of methodological production and use of the visual also points to Benjamin's (2008) concept of the dialectical image, a technique particularly suited for revealing temporalities of harm (and in particular, the sorts of environmental harm described more thoroughly in the following chapter).

As previously described in Chapters 1 and 2, the power of the image to establish truth—to reveal to us a given reality of our social condition—is intimately tied to the role of a non-academic popular criminology in constructing and configuring social knowledge of crime and harm. While it may be difficult for working criminologists to figure a world in which all people do not spend their time obsessing over the multivariate minutiae of crime and harm, that is precisely the case for most people. As Marshall McLuhan and Quentin Fiore (1967: 108) describe in their seminal and foundational explanation of the power of mediated visual communication: 'Most people find it difficult to understand purely verbal concepts. They suspect the ear; they don't trust it. In general we feel more secure when things are visible, when we can "see for ourselves ...".' Images, here, can be understood as something like the first tone of the alarm clock, the stimulus that initially shocks us into action. Harm, then, usually first knocks at the door of social knowledge as an image.

Here we might think of the ways in which public perceptions of a harm, crime, or crisis are plainly conditioned by images of harm, crime, and crisis; the spectators, put simply, react to the spectacle in ways that are at least somewhat determined by framing. An example here might include the ways in which the developed nations of the Global North responded to images of the famine that devastated Somalia in the 1990s. As Jacqueline Sharkey (1993) describes, the first images of the crisis picked up by American and European media outlets were of starving, malnourished, and emaciated children, and the immediate reaction to those images was for their audience to put pressure on political leaders in the United States (US) to intervene in the disaster. That intervention, of course, was poorly executed, and led to a new flow of images. This second wave of images—which depicted the body of a dead US soldier being dragged through the street and otherwise desecrated—though, almost immediately reversed the tide of public sentiment as media audiences in the US demanded that intervention be abandoned and the US withdraw entirely from its Somali mission, a withdrawal which then set the stage for the famine. It was the reversal of sentiment, of course, that led directly to the catastrophic withdrawal, just as previous public reactions to images of famine had driven the demand for action in the first place. It certainly seems, then, that 'images … can stir emotions and foster public outcry like no other means' (Zillmann et al 1999: 208; see also Sharkey 1993). Reversing the issue, geographer David Campbell (2007: 358) has noted that the United Nation's special representative for Sudan blamed the lack of international action to intervene in the famine in Darfur, in the mid-2000s, on the lack of photographs of the famine's victims in Western media, illustrating that if action is conditioned or otherwise driven by the image, so too is inaction. Christina Twomey (2012) further underscores the importance of the visual in these sorts of attention-building and perception-guiding moments, noting that there is a strong historical connection binding humanitarianism, atrocity, and photographs (along with other visual materials).

For a visual criminology that primarily produces its own images in the field of research (see generally Natali and McClanahan 2017, 2020; Redmon 2017, 2018; Ferrell and Van de Voorde 2010), the evidentiary implications of the image and its role in urging public action are quite clear. Images produced in the course of research might be employed as objects ripe for analysis, or as the same sort of evidence of engagement common in early anthropology and noted earlier; or, images produced in the field might serve a more public or outward purpose, wherein they function to grab attention or urge and audience towards some sort of social or political action. Finally, as noted previously, the criminologist who produces images in the field might find some unique new modes and ways of seeing simply by training the eye on the social or material landscape through a mediating lens.

Producing criminological images: photovoice methods

Of course, useful original images can also be produced in the course of research by parties other than the researcher. Here, visual criminology might employ the sorts of dynamic and interactive visual production processes of photovoice methods. Caroline Wang and Mary Ann Burris (1997: 369) describe photovoice as a method that was developed in response to theoretical insights in critical theory, feminist theory, and learning theory, one uniquely and overtly tailored to harness 'the immediacy of the image' in order to 'furnish evidence and promote an effective, participatory means of sharing knowledge' by placing cameras in the hands of participants rather than researchers. By enabling research subjects to produce their own images, or to guide the gaze of a researcher or research agenda towards the images that are most significant for subjects, photovoice methods provide the expected evidentiary power of original images as well as the same sort of insight into the lives of participants.

Because of its origins in feminist theory, and because of its unique ability to give voice to marginalized, invisible, or otherwise vulnerable populations, photovoice methods have been used extensively in feminist research agendas. In criminology, too, photovoice is clearly a favored visual method for those working with such groups and populations. Wendy Fitzgibbon and Camille Stengel (2018), for example, have used photovoice methods to investigate the lives of marginalized and often-invisible populations of women in the United Kingdom and Hungary. Photovoice methods were also an essential component of research I conducted on the intergenerational effects of environmental harm in the Appalachian coalfields of the US, largely because of its suitability for use with youth populations (McClanahan 2017; Wilson et al 2007).

Photovoice methods have been tested and proven in their utility in revealing important and often invisible populations and problems. More importantly, though, and as has been extensively described elsewhere (Wilson et al 2007; Duffy 2011; Kessi 2011; Budig et al 2018), photovoice methods have the potential, unique among methodologies, to significantly empower research participants or subjects, and to break down some of the barriers that traditionally exist between researcher and subject.

The criminological analysis of existing images

Although the production of original images—either for analysis or for more purely evidentiary purposes—is at the obvious core of a visual criminological agenda, it is not the most common form of visual criminology already in practice. Rather, it seems clear that the most routine and reliably present mode of criminological visual analysis is the analysis of existing images.

This variant of visual criminological method finds its foundations in developments across various fields of media and cultural studies. In criminology, it represents a tendency most apparent in cultural criminology, which has always given some serious consideration to the meaning and power of images (and, more generally, of the image itself) (see generally Hayward and Presdee 2010; Ferrell 2017). One of the many strengths of this approach is that the field from which relevant images might be drawn is so vast. Here, researchers are able to take their pick from the nearly endless archives of existing images of crime, harm, and justice as well as the unceasing streams of newly produced and disseminated images of those same phenomena.

The images drawn from these canons for analysis are also likely to themselves be representative of the diverse constellations of the visual: some are likely to be documentary or evidentiary, some are likely to be bureaucratic, functional, or administrative, some are likely to be entirely fictive, and some are likely to be artistic. In the following, I briefly consider each in turn, noting and describing some of the potential strengths and weaknesses embodied in each.

Let us begin with the documentary or evidentiary image. We can imagine these, for our purposes here, as those sorts of images hitherto discussed that primarily serve to document or otherwise serve as evidence of engagement. These are the images, much like those discussed thoroughly by Collier and Collier (1967), that tell us that a social phenomenon is occurring. These images serve manifold purposes in a visual criminological agenda, and thus take various forms and have various implications for visual criminological methodologies. One of the essential purposes of these sorts of images is to encourage social engagement with or recognition of a problem, harm, or phenomena. An example of this sort of methodological use is illustrated by Natali and McClanahan (2017), who argue that the visual has a uniquely significant power to establish temporal environmental change, harm, or crime (discussed more thoroughly in Chapter 4). Much research has shown that the proliferation of images is essential in raising awareness of and encouraging action on social problems, and so the criminological use of compelling images has the potential to contribute to meaningful social action. Of course, this form of visual criminology does not actually require significant analytical attention be given to the visual, only that visual data be included in order to illustrate the text.

As Luc Pauwels notes (2011), the analysis of existing images also benefits from their 'non-reactive' nature; rather than being produced in response to some force or problem or another, these images are more likely to be 'pure' in the sense that the conditions of their production are largely divorced from the conditions of their use. Put simply, these are pictures of things as they are. One potential pitfall or shortcoming, of course, is that the social realities of 'things as they are' are never so clear as the image might have us believe. Nevertheless, the analysis of these sorts of existing images will certainly continue to occupy a place in the visual criminological agenda.

The second tendency evident in the criminological analysis or use of existing images is similarly evidentiary, but expands its horizons in order to interrogate and implicate administrative power and justice. As discussed previously in this book, the landscape of the visual is a constantly contested field constituted by ongoing struggles over the power to control and define the force of the image. As plenty of others have described, the administrative power of the state—and, more particularly, the criminal justice apparatuses that constitute that power—asserts itself into being and power in large part through the visual. Examples of this tendency range from the sorts of cultural iconographies of punishment discussed previously by Brown (2009) and others (and later in this book, in Chapter 5)—which often include relevant images of the administrative and bureaucratic architectures of punishment and incarceration—to Katherine Biber's (2013, 2018) work, discussed previously, on the ways in which visual evidence haunts our perceptions of crime and justice in a sort of 'cultural afterlife'. Regardless of where we locate it, what is essential to this stream of visual methods within criminology is the careful analysis of images that reveal or reify some new meaning or dimension of administrative power. We might also keep in mind, as Jonathan Simon (2001: 1053; see also Simon 2007) reminds us, that images also play a meaningful role in the construction and maintenance of administrative state power, often serving to manufacture public consent and grant institutional legitimacy (more on this point later in Chapters 6 and 7 as it relates, respectively, to prisons and police).

One potential methodological strength of this approach is quite straightforward: images that are illustrative of administrative power are often located in formal archives. This should not be taken lightly, as anyone with meaningful experience in field-based research can attest to the difficulties of locating or even producing appropriate images. This approach might ameliorate some of those issues by offering the visual criminologist the benefit of archival organization and access. One possible limitation of this approach, meanwhile, is that it is only really attuned to a relatively small slice of the pie: it reveals its insights at the narrow intersection of the administrative state, its agents and the visual. Nevertheless, this method and tendency contributes significantly to the analytical enterprise of visual criminology.

Analyzing fictive images: visual criminology, cinema, and fine art

Next, let us consider the criminological analysis of purely fictive but still visual cultural productions. The most obvious avenue for the criminological engagement with fictive existing images is in the sort of film analysis undertaken by Rafter and Brown (2011), who insist that cinema 'most exemplifies' the relation between culture (including, of course, visual culture) and criminology and that it reveals a space in which the sort of popular criminology discussed throughout this book and academic criminology meet. Rafter and Brown go on to offer several examples of a criminologically informed and insightful film analysis. Throughout, the method of this analysis is clear, although not articulated in any didactic or overt way. Rather, the authors simply engage in the sort of analysis that is, by now, surely second nature to those working within the related disciplinary paradigms of cultural studies and film studies.

Other cultural criminologists have also considered cinema within the context of visual research (Hayward and Presdee 2010; McClanahan et al 2017). As I and others have noted elsewhere (see generally McClanahan et al 2017; Lam and Tegelberg 2020), mainstream cinema is increasingly, it seems, interested in climate change and other problems and the intersection of human and non-human worlds. While these authors have called on green criminology, in particular, to respond to this development by increasing analytical engagement with cinema, this recommendation might be extended to more branches of the criminological tree. For example, a criminological analysis of so-called 'cli-fi'—the emergent genre of climate change-oriented science fiction—might reveal, when conducted in the casual methodological framework exemplified by Brown and Rafter, any number of useful insights into the intersection of power, harm, and the material worlds in which crime and justice operate.

Of course, all of the images we encounter are not captured in the categories discussed here. Not only are the social and relational dynamics of crime and harm and justice conditioned in and by the visual economies of documentary and evidentiary images—what we might, at least for a moment, imagine as a field of relatively uninflected photographic images wherein complicating factors like artistic intent and patronage are able to be left relatively unconsidered—but also by visual arts outside of the bounds of documentary photography. Cinema, of course, also falls clearly under the umbrella of visual art, but the modes and methods of film analysis are, obviously, often quite different from modes and methods more plainly suited to the analysis of fine art, documentary or commercial photography, painting, illustration, and so on. Moreover, at least in the late-modern artistic epoch we currently find ourselves, cinema is a far more public, popular, and impactful mode of visual fine art than the other forms and modes discussed in this section like painting, art photography, and illustration.

Despite its centrality in the social imaginary of the visual, the analysis of fine art is relatively marginal within criminology. There are, though, some notable exceptions, including Piers Beirne's (2013, 2014, 2015, 2018) work on the paintings of William Hogarth (discussed in the following chapter), Ronnie Lippens' work on the ways in which governmentality manifests first in painting (2010), Eamonn Carrabine's work on the intersections of criminological inquiry and art history (2017) and Kate West's work on the intersections of visual and historical criminologies (West 2019), which all contribute significantly to efforts to focus the criminological gaze on fine art— and, in particular, Western canonical art and antiquities—in order to improve our understandings of the image and its historical intersections with crime, harm, and justice.

Of course, we should also bear in mind that the distinctions between so-called 'high' and 'low' cultures that is at the core of cultural notions of aesthetics bears just as much on criminology as it does on other disciplines. On this important distinction, it is probably enough here to simply note that high and low do not correspond with art and non-art. As John Fisher (2001) describes, the high–low distinction has more to do with the canonical position of a given piece of art[1] than it does with the presence or absence of any particular aesthetic qualities. Accordingly, we might simply imagine 'low' art as that which is not included in the Western canon. Suddenly, then, the field of visual art expands dramatically to include commercial images, popular modes of visual expression like graffiti and street art, and other images that we might broadly consider representative of 'low' art.

Visual criminology might also, then, attune itself to the unending waves of these sorts of commercial images that wash over our social worlds. Commercial images, product labels, mass-produced visual products, and more might each have just as much to offer to a visual criminology as more formal, canonical, or 'high' art. While not overtly concerned with the analysis of particular images, some criminological work on 'greenwashing'—the processes through which corporate interests conceal or obfuscate their role in environmental harm through the clever use of packaging and marketing—has been undertaken that already indicates criminological interest in the analysis of relatively mundane but immensely powerful visual fields like advertising.

Presenting criminological images

Any of the methods described in this chapter can contribute, obviously, to the design, execution, and construction of visual criminological research. How, though, might such research be packaged and disseminated to a relevant audience? In this final section, we address some of the ways that visual criminology has been constructed and packaged. Put simply, we consider the final product of the methods described and delineated earlier, including forms like photo essays, media installations, forms of digital storytelling, visual ethnographies, and more in order to think about how visual criminology might be expressed.

The most obvious answer to how visual data might appear in criminological projects is what I described in the previous chapter, following Young, as the 'marginal image', the image as object, which appears only as window dressing to illustrate a point. Here, though, these purely illustrative images have little more theoretical relevance than any other image—a chart, for example, or the simple pictures of prison cells, handcuffs, and courtrooms included in what seems like every available introductory criminal justice textbook—appearing in the margins of a paper or a textbook or a monograph. A thoughtful visual criminology, though, might find myriad other modes of scholarly expression. These modes of expression, though, will of course vary in suitability, depending on the sorts of images implied, the methods used, and the particular aims and goals of the researcher.

One available format for the presentation and expression of original criminological images is the 'photo-ethnography' or 'photo essay'. Cecile Van de Voorde (2012) offers a useful and robust framework for this form of criminological expression, insisting that the utility and appropriateness of including ethnographic photography in criminological research is 'undeniable'. Here, we might define photo-ethnography as a format in which pictures tell the sort of criminological story we might usually reserve for text, which, as Van de Voorde notes, suffers from an 'inertia' that photo-ethnography might work against.

While there are not many examples of this form of presentation within criminology, we might imagine this mode as resembling the photographic sections of Bourgois and Schonberg's (2009) *Righteous Dopefiend*, discussed more thoroughly in Chapter 5. There, the images captured by photographer Jeff Schonberg as he accompanied sociologist Philippe Bourgois into the lives of IV drug users in California's Bay Area, tell just as much about the conditions of life within that community as Bourgois' text. Alternatively, we might open the scope of our criteria even more in order to accept what we might think of as *accidental* public (see Loader and Sparks 2011; Brown and Rafter 2013) or popular (see Kohm and Greenhill 2011) criminological photo-ethnographies, such as the streams of images that proliferate in the wake of events like environmental catastrophes. As I discuss later in Chapter 4, those sorts of images—for example, the body of images that captured the scope of harms to the US gulf coast caused by the BP oil well disaster in 2010—can be read themselves as criminologically relevant and insightful. Similarly, drawing together prisons and environmental harms associated with coal extraction, Judah Schept has worked in the field with a photographer in order to produce criminological images during ethnographic research (Schept 2014; Schept and Frank 2015).

Documentary methods

Another available format for the expression of a visual tendency within criminology—and, again, one geared towards work that deals with the production of original images—is the sort of documentary criminology described earlier. Here, the criminologist acts in the field as filmmaker, while the images produced might be allowed to stand on their own, similar to the approach taken in the photo-ethnographic method of presentation described in the previous section. Or, as Redmon describes and illustrates, the use of a documentary method might be employed in order 'reanimate' the textual by 'yoking [text] to the visceral experience of audiovisual depiction' (2017: 358–9). The strengths of documentary criminology do not, though, stop at its significant ability to intervene in and enliven text; as Redmon (2017: 360) argues, the thoughtful production of documentary images in the criminological research 'generates meaning and crafts sensorial knowledge that exceeds … representational ethnography'.

Documentary criminology, as described by Redmon (2015, 2017, 2018) and Hayward (2017), is methodologically compelling in that it is not static, and instead seeks out, experiences, captures, and communicates the 'textures of actual criminal, harmful and transgressive activities in all their sensory richness' (Redmon 2017: 364). Similar to the sort of documentary photography previously taken up and favored by cultural criminologists (see generally Ferrell and Van de Voorde 2010; Natali and McClanahan 2017, 2020), documentary methods in visual criminology seek to enliven research agendas that might otherwise be 'sanitized' or otherwise 'divorced' from the 'sensory richness' of crime and justice informed by the essential cultural criminological notion of *verstehen* (Hayward 2017: 137; see generally Ferrell 1997b). Quoting Redmon, Hayward also reminds us that the 'documentary itself' is as much an 'act of cultural criminology' as its production, presenting another interesting opportunity in documentary criminology to allow for new and compelling questions of artistic intent and subjectivity to be analyzed in a unique way (Hayward 2017: 147).

The documentary criminology described here offers the opportunity to present criminological research in new and compelling ways. Moreover, documentary methods such as these have the unique potential to capture a much wider audience than traditional forms of criminological expression. These are both, though, relatively formal productions. However, in a contemporary mediascape that appears to find no end to its appetite for crime stories, we might strive for a disciplinary reimagining in which such productions like Netflix's *Making a Murderer* (2015) and *The Pharmacist* (2020) and the breakout podcast *Serial* (2014)—to name but a few of the wildly popular recent titles—are recast as presenting criminological insight. While trained criminologists might disagree with those insights—certainly, I expect that we all regularly shake our heads at popular perceptions of and perspectives on crime and justice such as those presented in true crime programs and films—we must recognize that they are all the same central and essential to the sort of popular or public criminology that is so entangled with the visual criminology discussed here.

Conclusion

While visual criminology has been largely dominated by qualitative tendencies, it is worth noting here that there is also ample room for a more quantitative or mixed-methods criminology of the visual. I want to draw some distinction, though, between a criminology of the visual and a visual criminology. The latter, as I see it, is the concern of this book: the criminological tendencies and formations that have emerged to make criminological sense of the visual, formations that have coalesced into a distinct subfield or orientation. The former, though—what we might simply call a criminology of the visual—has less rigid and dogmatic strictures and confines. Such a criminology of the visual has already, of course, emerged, evident in research that systematically codes films, for example, or in areas like situational crime prevention or other forms of geographic information system (GIS)-engaged research with a strong cartographic tendency. Indeed, it seems—and this should be taken, I think, as a significant positive— that an interest in the visual, or at the very least the recognition that the inclusion of visual data might make a given piece of research more compelling, is one of the rare points of commonality between qualitative and quantitative methodological camps.

4

Environmental Harm and the Visual

Introduction

Among the most important moments in the history of photography was the publication, between 1844 and 1846, of William Henry Fox Talbot's *The Pencil of Nature*. The collection, which was the first commercially published book to be illustrated with photographs, described Talbot's development of the process of calotype printing, which allowed for the mechanical and chemical capture of light, producing what were, for much of the collection's audience, the first photographic images they ever saw (Talbot 1989). The project included a collection of images that, somewhat remarkably, represents much of the spectrum of photographic subjects at play well over 150 years later: still lifes, portraits, architectural studies, and even slice-of-life or *vérité* images are all represented in Talbot's work. What I want to draw attention to here, though, is not the content of Talbot's work—as fascinating as it may be—but rather the title of that work. For Talbot, it seems, the relation between the photographic image and the 'natural' world (more on that shortly) was plainly evident, with photography at last delivering the ability to capture 'nature' as conceptualized as all that is not human. Capture, of course, also implies mastery or dominance, as made clear by Allan Sekula (1986: 4) when he noted that photography initially promised, in addition to its early juridical deployment discussed previously, 'an enhanced mastery of nature'. Human visions of 'nature', then—and particularly nature's forms and relations to the human and the social—have long been at the center of the power of images.

Just as our various interactions with and understandings of crime the criminal justice system writ large—to include, obviously, the sites with which this book is concerned—are constructed and conditioned by images and our encounters with images, so too are our interactions with and understandings of the natural environment. While green criminology has, since its inception in the 1990s, encouraged and engaged in the criminological exploration of harms and crimes affecting the natural environment, it has only more recently been significantly attentive to the visual. This chapter will make a case for the necessity of including the visual and visually attuned thinking within the green criminological paradigm, calling for a stream of green criminological thought that explicitly connects the environmental with the cultural and, most significantly, the visual. This work is, of course, already underway (see generally Brisman and South 2013, 2014, 2016; Ferrell 2013; McClanahan 2014; Brisman 2017a, 2017b; Natali and McClanahan 2017; Redmon 2018), but there nevertheless remains more to explore. This chapter considers some of the pressing environmental issues of our time—for example, droughts and water crises, species loss and declines in biodiversity, animal abuse, and climate change and its assorted harms—and the ways in which they have been—or might be—investigated or understood visually.

The vocabulary of 'nature'

Before we begin, I offer some brief notes and thoughts on the vocabulary that structures this chapter. In particular, I wish to draw critical attention to the categorical concepts of 'nature' and 'environment'. While volumes could be written about the ways we know and refer to the world around us—the world, that is, that humans have *affected* but not *built*—I wish simply to note here that we really only know that world as an abstracted 'nature', and that the vocabulary of 'nature' that we employ leaves much to be desired. Writers far more capable than I have grappled with the meaning of 'nature'—including Raymond Williams (1976: 219), who famously argued in *Keywords* that 'nature' is 'perhaps the most complex word in the [English] language'— and so I do not attempt any sort of comprehensive unpacking here. I note though—as what I feel is a matter of necessity—that thinking uncritically or unimaginatively about the non-human world as some vague nature not only forces an incomplete analysis, it risks reifying some deeply harmful ideas about the social and material organization of planetary life. 'Nature', in my estimation, is an incomplete and often-useless category, more a semiotic vessel for the excesses of unexplained phenomena than any meaningful thing or category of things. I say all of that, though, just to say this: in this chapter I refer to 'nature' *without* constantly noting and belaboring its fuzziness. This concession is, more or less, made necessary by the visual: as I will describe briefly later in this chapter, nature as a category and technology is and has been produced and refined by the visual mechanisms of culture and cultural production.

Green and visual criminologies: existing synergies

Like drugs, punishment, and police, problems of environmental crime and harm have generated a considerable amount of criminological attention. While criminologists have been slower to focus their concern on harms and crimes against nature, the growth of such scholarship has been significant.

In the 1990s, critical criminologists Lynch (1990) and South (1998) each made calls for a criminological agenda or perspective that would be attuned to harms and crimes affecting the non-human environment and non-human animals. These calls were answered with the emergence of 'green criminology', a perspective that does precisely what Lynch and South and others had suggested. In the decades since, green criminology has grown exponentially, breaking new ground and creating new and compelling lines of criminological thought. The field has largely stuck to its critical origins—it is, after all, oriented towards 'harm' rather than 'crime', and largely focuses on issues at the intersection of environmental and social justice—while focusing the criminological gaze on a range of environmental issues including climate change (White 2012a, 2012b, 2018a; Halsey 2013; McClanahan and Brisman 2015; White and Kramer 2015), wildlife trade and trafficking (Wyatt 2012, 2013; Sollund 2013, 2019; Nurse 2015; Goyes and Sollund 2016), water rights and harms to global water systems (McClanahan 2014, 2016; Johnson et al 2016; Brisman et al 2018), nonhuman victims (Flynn and Hall 2017; White 2018b), and a host of others.

In the late 2010s, green criminology—which had previously been understood, I suspect, as necessarily materialist in a way that allowed for culture to always take a backseat—took a cultural turn, urged forward by Nigel South and Avi Brisman, who called on the field to draw cultural dimensions of environmental harm into the analytical fold. While this call was answered in various ways (see generally Natali 2013, 2016; McClanahan 2014, 2019; Natali and McClanahan 2017; McClanahan and South 2020), the most notable for my purposes here are the efforts made by some green criminologists to establish a distinctly visual green-cultural criminology. Here the work of Lorenzo Natali is particularly useful, as it offers a schematic vision of what a visual approach to environmental crime and harm might look like. Noting that such an approach is, as mentioned previously, likely to 'find its natural habitat in the area where green criminology and cultural criminology meet', Natali employs an innovative and thoughtful photo-elicitation method, similar to those discussed elsewhere in this book, which allows research participants to have their responses to environmental change and contamination conditioned by exposure to images (Natali 2016: 3).

Another point of connection, already hinted at, that makes visual green criminology an intensely visual and public strand of the discipline is even more obvious: while we may rarely visually encounter prisons or drugs, or even police, in our day-to-day non-criminological lives, we are always immediately surrounded by and immersed in material environments and ecosystems. So, while prisons and other sites of punishment, drug users and drug economies, and certain dimensions of policing might be relatively invisible, no such invisibility is extended—or could ever be extended—to the non-human environment. It makes sense, then, that visibility and the visual constitute an important dimension of the criminological enterprise of studying harms to the environment.

Because green criminology's visual turn has been led primarily by those working explicitly at the intersection of green and cultural criminologies, it makes sense that much of this work represents the same sort of analytical engagement with visual cultural productions that makes up so much of the cultural criminological canon. Here we might read work that seeks to uncover environmental themes in traditional visual media as a form of visual green criminology.

Other green criminologists with cultural and visual tendencies, meanwhile, have developed and described at length a number of other methodological innovations and interventions uniquely suited to uncovering and analyzing environmental harm and crime. Because each of these tendencies has been described previously here and elsewhere (see generally Natali 2016; Natali and McClanahan 2017), I simply note here that there is a distinction made in the visual-green literature between a green criminology with images and a green criminology about images. The former, it seems to me, represents the sort of window-dressing approach discussed previously, while the latter represents a more daring, interdisciplinary, and cutting-edge approach. This is not to say, though, that the simple inclusion or superficial analysis of images is not generally complementary to the green criminological enterprise. Rather, the sorts of images that may be only superficial in other arenas might actually be uniquely suited to green criminological analytical agendas because of the unique ability of the image to leverage a sort of temporal certainty that can in turn inform and support claims of causality.

Still others working within the broader paradigm of green criminology have produced research that takes an approach informed by and concerned with the visual while not actually engaging with images at all. An example here is work by Robyn Bartel (2005) and myself and Tyler Wall (Wall 2016; Wall and McClanahan 2015) that considers the role of drone aircraft, satellite imaging systems, and other technologies that are increasingly being deployed to detect and document environmental harms. Here we can also point to the significance of aerial photography and other technologies for aerial visualization, a distinct state power that does significant heavy lifting in the construction of visuality (see generally Hippler 2017). By analyzing and contextualizing these intensely visual technologies and techniques, this research again highlights that visual criminology does not necessarily mean a criminology that 'uses' or even analyzes images. Rather, such approaches are illustrative of the myriad ways in which attention to the image itself, the context of its production, its use after capture, and even the technologies that make capture possible can inform and enrich any criminological agenda.

Finally, let us turn our attention to a fourth form that a visual green criminology has indicated it might take: media analysis. As the popular media landscape becomes increasingly saturated with the types of sensationalized or otherwise compelling 'true crime' programming discussed previously, it stands to reason that productions that capture or otherwise speak to contemporary ecological harms and problems will grow in number and salience. Here we can turn to Steven Kohm and Pauline Greenhill (2013), who make a convincing case that cinema and other visual forms of cultural production contribute to the construction of a popular criminology. Others still (McClanahan et al 2017), meanwhile, have offered a comprehensive consideration of the utility, scope, and mode of such an analysis for criminology. Because the media landscape appears to be increasingly populated with depictions of environmental harm and crime—largely, it would seem, as a result of increasing public awareness of the climate crisis—it is reasonable to assume that green criminology will continue down an increasingly visual path, and the conventional analysis of media will undoubtedly play a significant role.

Another compelling example of a traditional media analysis at the intersection(s) of criminology, the visual, and the given environment is recent work by Anita Lam and Matthew Tegelberg (2020), who encourage a visual green criminological agenda by raising questions of the co-constitution of environmental harms in the vanishing Arctic and the Anthropocene through traditional crime scene images. These authors make the point that the contemporary natural environment is itself a crime scene, and that anywhere we might look we are sure to find evidence of environmental harm, and so the trick is simply to attune ourselves to recognizing what we are seeing.

Images, evidence, and environmental change

In order to further pursue the connections between environmental harm and crime and the visual, it might be useful to first consider some fundamental connections between the visual image and the non-human world. The image, as described in Chapter 2, is still very much understood in the baseline criminological imagination as evidence. For the green-cultural criminological enterprise, the image may serve as evidence of environmental conditions, environmental harm, cultural responses and resistance to environmental harm, ecocide, and so forth. Indeed, many of these conditions may be only adequately communicated by the image—understanding the environmental changes that happen in the wake of industrial or extractive projects, for example, requires a visual form of what Walter Benjamin described as the 'dialectical image' (see Pensky 2004), a single image or composite that visually illustrates a historical dialectic, the passing of time and shifting material conditions. An image of what is materially and objectively an ecological harm—an image that captures one end of a temporal process—might not mean what it means, to a viewer detached from the temporal processes that gave rise to the harm, without being coupled with an image of the other end of that temporal line. Put simply, without understanding what once was, we can often not understand what is.

Part of this, it seems, is due to the universality of our (human) entanglement with the non-human worlds around us. No matter who or where we are, we are part of a broader environment, and our actions always implicate that entanglement. Here we can also briefly consider Timothy Morton's (2018) point that, like it or not, all human life and action is ecological, in the sense that all that we do (or fail to do, for that matter) triggers some sort of impact or effect in the given ecological world. Because those impacts are most readily recognized in the visible change of environments and ecosystems—at least for the layperson without the scientific training, tools, and inclination to investigate such harms at a less immediately visual level—we might then say that we know and understand our environment and any changes to it through an intensely visual relationship.

Images, media, and non-human animals

The evidence of causality and temporal relations described here makes it clear that images—whether captured on film, or by the eye—are or should be an essential component of knowing that an environmental harm has occurred. It seems that this is certainly the case when it comes to popular knowledge. Here we can again consider the essential point made by Rafter and Brown (2011) noted in previous chapters: criminological knowledge is coproduced by academic criminologists and the public audience of visual depictions of crime and harm. As I go on to describe, dramatic moments of environmental harm often capture significant public attention through the spread of images of the suffering of non-human animals, and so it seems sensible to say that an *academic* green criminology (particularly one with images) will likely intersect significantly with a *popular* green criminology. We might, then, make some effort to think critically and meaningfully about the moments in which the two converge, and how that convergence is particularly driven by and relevant for harms to non-human-built environments. It seems fitting, I think, that we might consider some of the distinct and discrete moments of environmental harm and crime that have captured significant criminological and public attention.

Let's begin with two of the most widely recognized and decried moments of environmental harm to have captured public attention in recent decades: the *Exxon Valdez* tanker spill in 1989, in which over 10 million gallons of oil were dumped into Alaska's Prince William Sound after the tanker's crew crashed the vessel into a reef, and the 2010 BP Deepwater Horizon disaster that in 2010 pumped over two hundred million gallons of oil into the Gulf of Mexico. In the case of the *Exxon Valdez* disaster, images of oil-soaked seabirds occupied the front pages of seemingly every newsstand publication, and airwaves and news reports were consumed for months with images of the cleanup. The BP disaster, meanwhile, caused a flood of published images (many also of oil-soaked seabirds, which sadly seem to be the photogenic stars of these sorts of tragic events) of oil slicks contained by floating booms and dispersed through the application of surfactant compounds. In both cases, the breadth and horror of the event was communicated visually, and it was the visual register that was temporarily entirely occupied with images of the disaster. After all, nobody (or so we might hope) enjoys seeing images of suffering marine life, but images of that suffering will nevertheless always outwork written, oral, or otherwise non-visual narratives in communicating that suffering.

Here we can turn our attention to another charismatic and photogenic animal that has come to symbolize an environmental crisis, the polar bear. Polar bears, of course, have long captured human attention and affection, most obviously illustrated in the example of the much-beloved Coca-Cola bears, which emerge from hibernation each December to play the role of cuddly soda mascots, enjoying their position as the apex talisman in the tundra of visual advertising. Somewhat ironic, then, that the other dominant image of the polar bear is distinctly different and countervisual; here, of course, I am speaking of the starving polar bear, its hip and shoulder joints showing clearly through a mottled pelt as it drifts helplessly on a floating sheet of ice, seemingly stranded there in the melting arctic by the forces of climate change (see generally Lam and Tegelberg, 2020). These two images serve as an environmentally focused illustration of Mirzoeff's 'countervisuality' (2011a, 2011b) discussed previously, in that the Coca-Cola bears and the gauzy arctic dreamworld they occupy present us with the dominant image, a glimpse of a planet unaffected by the human metabolization of the non-human. That world, of course, is a fiction, owing largely to interests like Coca-Cola, whose role in the crisis of global ecology cannot be overstated. The countervisual narrative—the desperate and suffering bear on the ice—is the far less pleasant reality of a global ecology undergoing the dramatic changes and crises wrought by the dominant modes of consumptive capitalism.

There has been some significant work in various fields of ecological study on the ways in which 'charismatic mega-fauna' (Skibins et al 2013) like polar bears capture the attention of the actors and institutions we might understand, for our purposes here, as constituting the 'environmentalist' movement. This category of animals includes those creatures with which humans seem exceptionally willing to identify and those animals—generally large—that otherwise capture human attention. It seems obvious, though, that these moments of identification, interest, and attraction are largely undertaken in the arena of the image. It is, then, not simply that visual inputs often inform us of environmental changes, but that the emotive and affective conditions of human–environment relations (and, more particularly, relations between humans and non-human animals) are dictated—or, at least, informed—by the images we take in.

Another example of this can be located in social responses to the bush fires that, driven by climate change-induced drought (Yu et al 2020) and various programmatic political failures, devastated Australia in 2019. Prior to the COVID-19 pandemic, of course, images of the fires were everywhere in the media landscape; heart-stopping pictures of crowds of fleeing people gathered on beaches, of the usually lush and verdant landscape transformed into a smoldering hellscape, of charismatic fauna like kangaroos and koala bears fleeing or perishing, or of fatigued firefighters working against the impossible conditions of the burn, which ultimately consumed nearly 50 million acres of the continent (Tin et al 2020). Within this new visual landscape—one that emerged fully formed almost immediately concurrent with the fires gaining global media attention—though, there was one type of image that seemed to transcend the power of the rest. These, the images of suffering animals (and, more particularly, koalas and kangaroos), seemed to at least momentarily capture the full messy contents that constituted the disaster (Hope 2020).

Anyone paying attention to our reactions to images of non-human suffering, of course, could be forgiven for wondering why non-human suffering seems to produce images that have far more social and political potency than images of human suffering, such as the images from the US torture program at Abu Ghraib discussed in Chapter 2 or the images of drug addicts discussed in the following chapter. This is, at least in some part, explained by the ways in which humans—and, in particular, criminalized, gendered, and racialized others—are often non-ideal victims. The 'archetypal image of (Western) society's "ideal" or "legitimate" victim is embodied by a young, innocent female' who is 'out doing good deeds when she is attacked by an unknown stranger', while such ideal victims of crime are those most likely to generate media attention and 'arouse sympathy from the public at large because they are deemed to be blameless' (Lam and Tegelberg 2020: 109). Non-human victims like polar bears, seabirds, and fire-singed kangaroos and koalas, though, have none of the baggage of race and gender and class and culpability;[1] they are largely free of blame, and so spectators are far more likely to be meaningfully stirred by images of their suffering.

Unfortunately, though, it appears that whatever action is encouraged by images of animal suffering is not enough. After all, one only need to flip or click through the contemporary mediascape to see that we are constantly bombarded with images of non-human suffering, and so it is plainly evidently that our displeasure with such images has not resulted in an end to harms against animals.

Animals like polar bears, though, do not only emerge in our visual cultures as victims, ideal or otherwise. Just as with all other images, context and framing are powerfully determinant when it comes to the way that spectators receive and respond to the spectacle. An example of the ways in which context, framing, and the aesthetic qualities of an image condition our response can be found in another moment in which polar bears crashed into the public imagination. In December of 2018, over 50 polar bears began to converge in Belushya Guba, a town on the Russian Novaya Zemlya archipelago in the Arctic Sea. The bears, which were drawn to the town's garbage dumps after years of decreasing sea ice and attendant food shortages, quickly became the new non-human stars of a visual drama when they began to roam the streets of the town and, on at least one occasion, enter residents' homes.

In this story, though, the bears were not the cuddly soda variety, nor the suffering and stranded '#sickbear' social media star described by Lam and Tegelberg. Instead, the bears of Belushya Guba were cast in a *vérité* eco-horror picture, their ghostly and hulking frames scouring for food and terrifying residents and outside spectators. Just like that, the charismatic ursine victims of our climate crisis were transformed from protagonist to antagonist, like they went from a cartoon Mickey Mouse character to Hannibal Lecter, the iconic fictional serial murderer in *The Silence of the Lambs* (1991), in the blink of an eye. Gone, more or less, were any concerns about anthropogenic climate change and the role of human activity in producing non-human suffering, despite the fact, of course, that it was those same factors that produced both #sickbear and the bears of Belushya Guba. Like other images, and other images of suffering, images of non-human suffering are contested and contingent, conditioned by a constellation of forces that includes history, politics, and capital.

Capturing images of nature

A key and critical legal issue raised in the capture of images of non-human animals concerns questions of property, ownership, and self-determination. These issues are most notably and clearly at work in the example of legal disputes that arose around images of Celebes crested macaque monkeys taken—or, as we will learn, perhaps not taken—by British nature photographer David Slater. In 2011, Slater—who had for several years taken regular trips to Indonesia to photograph crested macaques, a species with a distinctly expressive face that is, at the risk of endorsing a plainly subjective judgement, remarkably charming—released a tranche of images of crested macaques through a news agency for selective publication in British media (Abbott 2020). The images were accompanied by a press release, in which Slater described the conditions under which the images were produced. In that press release, Slater noted that many of the images had been produced when the inquisitive monkeys had been captivated by their reflections in the camera's lens, and that the monkeys themselves had operated the wired shutter release. Indeed, this was the narrative that accompanied the images, which were almost immediately a hit with the British public and seen as a potentially significant boost to efforts to conserve the habitat of the Indonesian crested macaques because they established the monkeys as charismatic characters (more on non-human charisma and its relation to the visual to follow shortly).

The images, then, were not strictly taken by Slater: while it was his camera, the moment of lenticular capture—which is, of course, the most decisive and permanent moment in the chain of events that produce a photographic image—was initiated by the monkeys themselves. These images were not the work of the acclaimed photographer Slater. No, these were something quite different indeed: monkey selfies. Five days after the initial release of the images by Slater and the Caters News Agency, the selfies—which ultimately comprised only a small number of the total images released—were uploaded to Wikimedia Commons, a publicly accessible website dedicated to hosting and archiving materials that are under free-use license, public domain, or are otherwise unable to be copywritten. The individual who uploaded the images to Wikimedia Commons included a note that they were 'the work of a non-human animal' and that as such there was no human interest into which ownership of the images was vested. Slater challenged the fair-use status of the images, insisting that his role in the production of the images was sufficient to imply copyright, with arguments concerning even the most seemingly trivial details (for example, much debate was made over how many fingers Slater had on his tripod when the macaque pressed the shutter, and the particular social role that Slater held within the troop of macaques), but ultimately lost. The images remain in the public domain, with the US Copyright Office affirming the position taken by Wikimedia Commons, which hosted and distributed the images: because a non-human animal cannot be granted legal copyrights, images taken by a non-human animal must necessarily be in the public domain. Slater was also sued by the animal rights organization People for the Ethical Treatment of Animals for including the images in a commercially available book. This second case was resolved in a 2018 decision in which a judge affirmed the earlier view that non-human animals were unable to hold copyright, but where the earlier decision held that as a result images produced by non-human animals were not able to be copyrighted, the second judge held that copyrights over such images could legally be granted to human actors, provided their role in the production was sufficiently necessary (as, the judge ruled, Slater's had been).

This case—and other similar cases sure to come in its wake—highlights the various ways in which images and the visual might increasingly lie at the heart of tensions between humans and non-humans, and between human groups and movements pursuing the liberation of animals and groups and movements working to maintain vertical and hierarchical relations between the human and non-human.

The role of images in environmental justice

It is not surprising that human groups resisting harms to animals are often characterized by their use of the visual. Visual cultural products routinely play a distinctly and intensely significant role in the resistance to environmental harm and crime. Here, we might again turn to green-cultural criminology as the disciplinary variant most suited to analyze the relation between environmental harm and the visual. As Brisman and South (2013, 2014) describe, green-cultural criminology—or, more precisely, the visual green-cultural criminology called for by myself, Natali, and others—is particularly well suited to an analysis of the ways in which environmental harm, crime, change, and contamination are resisted because much resistance is socially organized and communicated using images.

Here we can consider the ways in which images of environmental harm themselves might be mobilized in order to resist harm. Perhaps one of the most salient and noteworthy examples here is in campaigns for animal rights, campaigns which often employ an aesthetic mode that connects them to other corpuses of images of suffering. Many readers have, no doubt, encountered protesters or posters or billboards which, in the name of animal liberation, depict or otherwise visually illustrate practices like animal vivisection, slaughter, testing, or other forms of harm and torture. The logic of the strategy is clear: in order to get people to care about harms to animals, they—the people—must be shocked into action, and what better way to shock them than to expose to them the visceral reality of the harm. What little research into the actual symbolically interactive processes at play in these interactions there is indicates that images of environmental harm and injustice play a crucial role in the formulation of social movements to resist those harms (Flores et al 2011). Even if, it seems, there is widespread social knowledge of environmental harm, socially organized resistance to harm is only likely when the harm is communicated visually.

This was evident in the circulation of images, for example, of fires—many intentionally set in order to hasten the displacement of resistant populations of humans and non-humans—in the Brazilian Amazon.

For weeks, in late 2019, images of the fires circulated online and in print media. On social media in particular, the images were shared expressly, it seems, in order to rally a global network of occasional activists to apply political pressure to Brazil's newly inaugurated right-wing government, which many blamed for the fires. Suddenly, the health of the Amazon was on every agenda—or at least every social media feed—despite previous moments of environmental devastation in the rainforest that had gone largely unaddressed in Northern concerns (such as deforestation, earlier fires, water pollution).

Art and the cultural production of nature

While criminologists often talk of 'landscapes', we rarely do so literally. We talk about horizons, too; the series in which this book appears promises to explore new horizons in criminology, and I certainly use the word 'landscape' throughout in order to refer to the conceptual landscape of things like disciplines and modes and forms of thought. A green criminology, of course, must be more mindful and material in how it approaches and conceptualizes landscape, although even there it is not a strictly material category. A visual criminology of environmental harm, though, is naturally urged to consider landscapes as an artefact of both immaterial cultural production, on the one hand and, on the other, the material and given world.

Landscapes, like nature, are not exactly a consistently fixed or real thing, yet they are imbued with a nearly unimaginable cultural and political power and, perhaps more importantly, the very concept and category of landscape conditions our perceptions of the non-human world. The power of landscape as a technology is largely in its role in the production of 'nature' as a category outside of the human with which we might interact, an aesthetic with a focus on the countryside where 'evidence of human labor can be erased or hidden' (Neumann 2003: 240). Prior to the global development of landscape as a category in art, most representational art had been largely preoccupied with human and animal subjects, with 'landscape' relegated entirely to the background of images. When that attention shifted, though, the change was seismic (albeit slow, given the limitations in global exchange that characterize pre-digital visual cultures). In Eastern art histories, landscape emerged as a form early, particularly in China, where 'the great subject' of painters was landscape, while 'the first climactic accomplishments in that category were achieved from the tenth to twelfth centuries' in China (Lee 1954: 199). In Western histories, the mode of landscape came to the fore more slowly, with the sorts of picturesque landscape we are all familiar with today rising to the fore with the advent of pre-Victorian English gardens in the mid-18th Century (Czerniak 1997).

Well before the dawn of photography, landscape had been a central category of the visual. In America, painters like Thomas Cole and other figures of the Hudson River School movement in the early 19th century produced landscapes that portrayed the rugged terrain of the eastern US in romantic grandeur, while others like Albert Bierstadt and Thomas Moran painted the landscapes of the Western American frontier in the mid-19th century, with Bierstadt favoring a bright luminist style and Moran favoring a darker and more dramatic tone. Just as earlier and parallel developments and movements in art produced images that reflected and reified the sorts of racialization, gender violence, and oppression of the day, however, so too did landscape painting. Early paintings of the landscapes of the western US, for example, simply omitted all signs of Indian life, and both European and early American landscape movements have been rightly criticized for their role in producing masculine domination as a force of 'nature'.

Figure 4.1: Thomas Cole's *View from Mount Holyoke, Northampton, Massachusetts, after a Thunderstorm—The Oxbow*, 1836

Note: This painting is emblematic of the style of landscape favored and popularized by Cole and other artists of the Hudson Valley School. Such images also played a crucial role in constituting the visual figure of 'nature' in the US and Europe.

Source: Courtesy of Mrs Russell Sage.

In the colonial world, meanwhile, landscape painting came to be a way in which the white colonial vision might be set apart from indigenous visions. In what is, for my money, the most lucid illustration of the power of visuality, as conceptualized by Mirzoeff and as described in Chapter 2, the painted colonial landscape was a technology of differentiation, a way in which white settlers and colonial states could assert their sole mastery over history and preclude other ways of seeing and forms of knowledge. As Roderick Neumann describes, the landscape was an essential technology and technique of colonial power well into the 20th century, when it was instrumental in establishing Serengeti, the first National Park in British-ruled Africa. As Neumann notes, the colonial vision of African land mirrored colonial ideas about African people, with both existing with a conceptual tension, in the colonial imagination, between production and consumption: in land, the new ideology of preservation (informed largely by landscape art) clashed with desires to transform African resources into English capital, while in culture the colonial imagination wrestled with competing visions of Africans as romantically primitive 'noble savages' and, conversely, as purely untapped labor (Neumann 2003: 241). It was what Denis Cosgrove calls (following John Berger's [2008] seminal *Ways of Seeing*, discussed in Chapter 2) the landscape 'way of seeing' that ultimately most informed these earlier colonial visions of the world, and it was likewise these traditions and images that produced what endures as the dominant Western idea and ideology of 'nature'. For a visual criminology interested in the processual dimensions of the image and of seeing, the history of landscape painting and its role in domination and power provides an important insight into the ways that cultural images have material power over human–environment interactions.

Since prehistory, animals have also played an important role in art. From poetry to theater, and from painting to photography, animals have long been among the favored subjects of artists and art consumers alike. Francis Klingender (2019) exhaustively described the ways in which animals other than humans populate folklore, art, and literature, and the ways in which humans have, through that inclusion, used the non-human as a screen on to which we might project our desires or anxieties. Joining Klingender in that recognition and offering his own account of the animal turn in the graphic arts, Piers Beirne (2013, 2014, 2018) has offered a non-speciesist criminological reading of the ways in which animals—and, more importantly in his analysis, harms to animals—play a crucial social role in the engravings of 18th-century English artist William Hogarth. Beirne's approach here is also instructive both stylistically and methodologically for a visual criminology of animals in art, as he exhaustively mines and analyzes Hogarth's paintings, placing their representations of animals in their historical and social context. This approach to reading images of non-human animals is deeply reliant on the knowledge and methods of art history and criticism, but it is also potentially deeply revelatory, as is Beirne's work on Hogarth, in that it can reveal important insights into the ways in which images are produced and imbued with meaning through social processes, and how social processes, in turn, are acted on by the visual.

This stream of thinking also reminds us that that images which impact relations between animals and humans are not necessarily fine art, either. Rather, we encounter non-photographic images of non-human animals—and, of course, other dimensions of nonhuman nature—all of the time. From children's cartoons to graphic arts, product packaging to fashion trends, we are surrounded by images of nature that are entirely artificial. Finally, then, turning from fine art to commercial art, we might also consider the phenomenon of corporate 'greenwashing', a technique in which products are packaged in ways that encourage consumers to feel positive about the environmental impacts of the products they consume (Delmas and Burbano 2011; Ferrell 2013; Nurse 2014). A classic example of this is surely familiar to us all, the single-use plastic water bottle with a colorful label depicting a pristine landscape and a cascading waterfall. Never mind, of course, what we know about the consequences of the bottle: it is produced using vast quantities of fossil fuels, it is unlikely that the water it contains is any better than the tap water you can consume for a fraction of the cost, and it will ultimately only contribute to the crisis of global water pollution that the label takes such pains to obscure. Both of our options—the choice to consume in ways that are harmful to non-human nature and the choice to resist harming non-human nature—are deeply affected by the visual.

Methods in visual green criminology

Before concluding, let us take a moment to consider more carefully the ways in which the visual tendencies already expressed by green criminology take shape methodologically. As previously mentioned, Natali and McClanahan (2017) draw some distinction between a green criminology *with* images and a green criminology *about* images. The former is most clearly embodied in Natali and McClanahan's (2017) photo-elicitation method; this approach allows for images to structure and complement the sociological investigation of environmental harm and change. The latter, meanwhile—a visual green criminology about images—centers the image as the site(s) of its analysis. This approach is most evident in research that turns to the content of visual cultural productions in order to uncover insights into the intersection(s) of environmental harm and the social world, or that produces images of its own in order to establish a distinct temporality or causality (see generally McClanahan 2019).

Other methods of engagement with the visual suitable for green criminology are those used by Bartel (2005) and others (see generally Wall and McClanahan, 2015) that consider the intersections of non-human animals and environments, the anthropocentric social world, and the techniques and technologies of the visual. This sort of research does not particularly require the production nor the analysis of images, only that the researcher remain attuned to the evidentiary and political power of the image and the ways in which the context of its production might themselves uncover new knowledge at the intersection of the social and environmental worlds.

Finally, there is the innovative method offered by David Redmon. His documentary criminology, discussed elsewhere in this book, is an exciting and cutting-edge complement to those discussed in this chapter. Its utility and potential as an addition to the methodological toolbox of the visually attuned green criminologist has already been proven by Redmon's exploration of the lives of donkeys. Redmon, who argues convincingly that his method is uniquely capable of adding a 'sensuous' dimension to the production and tenor of criminological knowledge (more on this later as it relates to the development of 'sensory criminology' that has emerged alongside and in response to visual criminology), plays both sides, producing the visual product itself (in this case, a documentary film) and then analyzing the conditions and results of its production.

Conclusion

The significance of Talbot's (1989) pencil of nature for the development of photography is clear. We should again consider, though, what this tells us. As this chapter has shown, the relationship between the visual image and the non-human ecological world is both elemental and intensely constitutive: we know our environments and the human and non-human animals that populate them in visual ways. We know harms to those environments have happened often only because we are able to visually perceive environmental change. We make and consume images of animals and non-human nature, even as we understand that that consumption might sometimes harm non-human animals and nature.

We also, though, respond with care and empathy when confronted with images of harm and the suffering of the non-human. We take careful precautions, at times, to ensure the rights and autonomy of animals. We treasure and cherish images of the natural world and its non-human inhabitants, and we feel the painful sting of empathy and the desire to act in images of non-human suffering. This chapter has described some of those dynamics, and some of the ways that criminology—in particular green and green-cultural criminologies— have responded to them. Moving forward, green criminology and visual criminology will likely only grow closer. As lay and public understandings of the global climate crisis and other emerging ecological crises inevitably grow, we will likely begin to see more thought and action at the intersection of the visual, the ecological, and the criminological.

5

Drugs and the Visual

Introduction

Of all of the social problems associated with crime and justice, perhaps none occupies space on the registers of visual culture like the problem of drugs. Long a central site and locus of criminological inquiry, drugs and the related issues they give rise to have always been essential characters in the drama of crime and justice, and those dramas largely play themselves out in the field of the visual image. From the menacing image of the crazed marijuana user immortalized in the film *Reefer Madness* (1936) to contemporary visual productions like popular 'Faces of Meth' campaigns, drug trends and associated issues and problems are constructed and communicated, reified, and even fabricated and cut from the whole cloth of the visual. The visual world(s) of drugs is also perhaps the best and most salient available example to illustrate the sort of flexibility and 'unfixedness' of images and aesthetics, the way that images and visual cultures have their meanings negotiated by the social processes that constitute the practice of seeing.

This chapter surveys the various ways in which drugs are given life and meaning in the visual registers of crime and culture, what might be learned or uncovered from those meanings, and the various—and, in the case of drugs, considerable—moments in which an explicitly visual criminology has already begun to engage with the specter of drugs. Among the most immediately relevant dimensions of drugs in visual culture, for a visual criminology, are important questions of ethics, representation, framing, power, and meaning, and so those are the questions to which we now turn.

Drugs, cinema, and media

Like police and prisons, drugs play an essential—and intensely visual—role in constructing the image(s) of crime, harm, and justice that inform the social imagination. Indeed, among the very first films ever produced was a roughly 30-second silent kinetograph called *Chinese Opium Den* (1894). Unsurprisingly, the film—which was commissioned by none other than the renowned American inventor Thomas Edison and filmed by photographer W.K. Laurie Dickson—depicted, simply, a Chinese man smoking opium. Underscoring the remarkably enduring tendency of cinematic depictions of drugs and drug users, it is worth mentioning that *Chinese Opium Den* was produced in the spring of 1894, mere months after Edison filed the first formal copyright request for a film, in January of 1894, for *Kinetoscopic Record of a Sneeze*, a film he had commissioned in late 1893 (Starks 2015: 13).

Drugs, then, have been a cinematic subject for as long as cinema has existed, and there is, as a result, a robust visual economy of drug images and media. Indeed, this relation was almost certainly the source of the first controversies surrounding obscenity and cinema and other forms of contemporary media: only five short years after the production of *Chinese Opium Den*, anti-drug and anti-obscenity crusader and publishing magnate William Randolph Hearst's *New York Journal* called moving picture cinemas 'picture galleries of Hell' that trafficked in images 'too vulgar to be described' (quoted in Siff 2015: 19–20).

Since arriving on the cinematic scene, drugs have conditioned and configured characters and sets and settings and stories. Many of popular visual culture's biggest stars emerge from the mediated and visual worlds of drugs. In cinema, protagonists like *Scarface*'s (1983) Tony Montana and *Goodfellas*' (1990) Henry Hill both constructed and immortalized the violent paranoia of the archetypical cocaine-addicted drug boss, while films such as *Up in Smoke* (1978), *Dazed and Confused* (1993), and *Half Baked* (1998) construct, in the social imagination, the visual figure of the 'stoner' and, along the way, the genre of 'stoner cinema'. Heroin and methamphetamine, for what it's worth, appear to be less readily romanticized in cinema, with their representation largely limited to the sorts of bleak scenes imagined in films and television series like *Breaking Bad* (2008), *Drugstore Cowboy* (1989), *Winter's Bone* (2010), and *Trainspotting* (1996). Alcohol, of course, is a persistent presence across visual media, and cinema is no exception, and films like *Leaving Las Vegas* (1995) have surely contributed significantly to the image of the alcoholic in the public imagination. Other visual media, too, are of course implicated in this process, with everything from commercial and art photography, advertising, graphic and industrial design, and digital and print media contributing to the visual and visible images of drugs and drug users that configure their social and cultural position and meaning. From the opium den, to the speakeasy, to the crackhouse, to the traphouse, the stories favored in visual cultural registers (of cinema and more) are routinely set in spaces and places constructed by drugs and populated by characters who use, sell, or are otherwise involved in illicit drugs and drug economies. From the silly to the serious, though, an immutable fact remains: drug addicts, dealers, manufacturers, and the cops that hound them are all constructed, in the mind's eye of the social imaginary, from a patchwork of mediated visual images.

Drugs and addiction portraiture

Among the most essential and powerful images of drugs, images that are picked up and reproduced in cinema, are those created by fine art and documentary photographers. Since at least the middle of the 20th century, art photographers and documentarians both have captured images from the lives of drug users. The resulting images, far from the glittering wealth-fantasy of *Scarface* (or, at least, the middle third of the film) are generally considered to be realist in their nature, although it is important to note that such realist images must always wrestle with a vision of 'authentic' drug images that tells the social imaginary how drug images should look. Here, I am not particularly concerned with tracing the origins of those establishing images, but with seeing the ways in which they condition this form of image. We should keep in mind, then, that our deeply and dearly internalized vision of the realities of addiction are little more than echoes of the images of addiction we are already familiar with.

In the mid–1950s, American photographers like Gordon Parks—a true renaissance man who worked variously as a photographer for the Farm Security Administration (FSA), and as a poet, writer, musician and composer before ultimately going on to direct 1971's *Shaft*, a film widely considered to mark the birth of the blaxsploitation genre— trained their cameras on, among other criminal actors, drug addicts in the growing inner cities of America. For Parks, this tendency culminated in *The Atmosphere of Crime*, a series he shot for *Life* magazine and which was run in 1957 as an eight-page color photo spread capturing various images from the worlds of crime and justice. Central to the spread are images of drug users—and, in particular, users of intravenous drugs, often photographed in the act of injection. Parks' drug images in the series are deeply significant in the development of contemporary documentary photography, almost certainly influencing the ways in which subsequent artists would wrestle with the visual worlds of drugs and drug use (see generally Donloe 1993). Parks himself, of course, was undoubtedly influenced by Arthur Fellig, who under the pseudonym Weegee produced a body of images in the 1930s and 1940s— in particular, of often gruesome crime scenes—while working as a press photographer in New York City's Lower East Side.

Weegee's work focused less on drugs and more on death and violence than Parks', and has garnered some attention in visual criminology (see generally Carrabine 2012, 2015, 2016; Biber 2015; Lam 2021). Like Parks, too, the realism of Weegee's images would be picked up in the cinematic world of the moving image, with Fellig going on to work in collaboration with acclaimed directors Stanley Kubrick and Jack Donohue while his photographic work had a significant influence on artists including Diane Arbus and Gary Winogrand, who are each, in their own rights, deeply important in the development of the sorts of images considered by visual criminology.

Following Parks, a host of other fine art photographers would emerge, cameras at the ready, to capture the lives of drug users. Notable contributors to the genre of documentary drug photography include Larry Clark, who like Parks would go on to work amid great controversy as a director, most notably of *Kids*, the 1995 film that brought images of 1990s' New York youth street culture to the world and which is itself, in part, a document of drug use. Clark's *Tulsa*, a collection of black-and-white photographs published in 1971, is particularly influential: its aesthetics represent a shift away from the soft color of Parks' crime images. Where Parks shot images that retain some of the aesthetic sensibilities cultivated during his time with the FSA, sensibilities which signal a certain documentary quality to his images, *Tulsa* is populated with similar figures (that is, drug users) shot in an entirely different way. In some critical sense, it feels as though Clark's images lack a sensitivity that is always evident in Parks' images. Part of this aesthetic distinction can, of course, be chalked up to differences in each artist's technical decisions: Parks' crime images are shot largely in color, while Clark's are entirely in black and white. Because of the differences in audience response to these two distinct modes of photography, and because there is, it seems, a unique relation that connects empathy, visual communication, and drug addiction, we can simply note that while Parks and Clark plainly exist along the same continuum of artistic practice, and while they both made photographs of intravenous drug users in the throes of addiction, the meanings and knowledge embedded in their respective images are nevertheless divergent.

Other photo essays of drug use and users, of course, have followed Parks and Clark, with the form seemingly retaining huge popularity among artists and audiences alike. Some notably popular examples include *Faces of Addiction*, by New York banker-cum-photographer Chris Arnade, which illustrates the daily lives of addicts—largely heroin and crack users—in the Bronx's Hunts Point neighborhood, and James Nachtwey's *The Opioid Diaries* (2018), which made up a special issue of *Time* magazine. Even some non-photographer academics have contributed to this particular body of drug images, such as Philippe Bourgois and Jeff Schonberg's, whose *Righteous Dopefiend* (2009) is discussed at several points in this book, and criminologist Heith Copes and photographer Jared Ragland, who have collaborated on a number of projects surrounding images of the lives of rural methamphetamine users. Constituting this corpus are what we might think of as examples of 'addiction portraiture', a genre united and recognizable—as all others—by shared aesthetic tendencies.

The potential of images, like Ragland's photo in Figure 5.1, made in the aesthetic frame offered by addiction portraiture to encourage an empathic response, is also clear in images made by photographer John Ranard. Ranard, who is most widely recognized for his photographs of boxers and boxing in Louisville, Kentucky in the 1970s and 1980s, also shot several series of images of HIV and AIDS-positive intravenous drug users in the grim, isolated infectious disease wards of Russian and Ukrainian hospitals and prisons. While he describes Ranard's images as situated within the tradition of drug photography associated

Figure 5.1: *Willow, 37* by Jared Ragland

Note: This photograph, by Jared Ragland, shows a woman through a mirror injecting intravenous drugs. Ragland's work on this subject is emblematic and illustrative of the compelling aesthetic tendencies of addiction portraiture and of the ways in which textual context can ameliorate some concerns over reductionism and other ethical issues embedded in the form.

Source: Courtesy of Jared Ragland.

with Clark's *Tulsa*—a tradition Fitzgerald (2002) quite accurately describes by noting its obsession with 'exposing in gruesome detail the horrible limits of human suffering and the primitive conditions of the drug user', which produces images that while possibly difficult to define, are easy to recognize—Fitzgerald focuses his attention on what marks Ranard's images as different from the genre to which they belong. Fitzgerald notes that images made in the stock aesthetic mode of this genre sometimes have, despite their claims of realism, a flattening effect: because of the connection of these images to 'profound ontological suffering', he writes, 'there is little place for the complexity and perhaps contradictory dimensions to drug use that may involve pleasure' (2002: 379). Fitzgerald is right, too: Ranard's images possess an entirely different set of qualities and elicit an entirely different response than many of their drug portraiture counterparts. Ranard's photos document all of the suffering of images made by other addiction photographers, but never take on the voyeuristic feel of his contemporaries. Ranard's subjects, as Fitzgerald describes it, 'have dignity, they have clothes and sleep in beds' (2002: 378). His images also eschew some of the common scenes and settings of the genre: there are no closely shot graphic images of injection, no blood and no gore. There is, however, ample human suffering, mixed, as it is in lived experience, with dignity and compassion.

There are also, however, some examples of drug images from within the fine art world that, in some meaningful way or another, more immediately contravene the aesthetic conventions of the genre. Here we can consider the work of fine art photographer Les Baker V, whose *INEBRI-NATION* (n.d.) project eschews the grim and dingy settings of Clark and the familiar realism of Parks, opting instead for manically bright and energetic pictures, shot in extreme close-up, of the faces of drug users in the moment in which they 'peak' on their drugs of choice, images of which are projected on to the subject's face. Artists like Graham MacIndoe, meanwhile, retain the basic aesthetic language of suffering and addiction that speaks in the images of Parks and Clark—all of the suffering and dinginess is very much present—but reverse the gaze: in MacIndoe's pictures, the artist is the addict, as he captures his own suffering in agonizing detail and clarity.

Although these images might have some capacity to communicate harm and suffering in such a way that results in some intervention, solidarity, or relief of the individual and social pains of addiction, there is of course no guarantee—and, in fact, no real reason to assume—that they will. Describing what he calls the 'dangerous rhetoric and imagery of "the opioid crisis"', critic Baynard Woods (2018) notes that images made in the mode of addiction portraiture, it seems, are alone in their representation of illness and disease. More importantly, though, Woods also describes how photos by luminaries in the genre like Clark and, later, Nachtwey, 'turn the users into grotesque victims and their dealers into mass murderers'. While the reception and meaning of an individual image are by and large subjective processes, of course, we can nevertheless note that the critique of these images leveled by Woods and others—that they essentialize and flatten their subjects into one-dimensional figures that may perhaps shock us but rarely challenge our assumptions about people affected by drug addiction—indicates that the aesthetic forms they reflect are inextricably bound to the social and political perspectives they engender and encourage; importantly, as Woods describes, this corpus of images is often called into service in the justification of draconian and harmful drug policies that only reproduce suffering and harm.

Not all drugs, though, implicate the types and degrees of suffering so evident in this hugely significant body of drug images. There are also, of course, visual dimensions of drugs and drug crime that are lighthearted, fun, and as full of life and joy as images by Parks, Clark, and MacIndoe are full of death and suffering. Drugs, after all, were instrumental in ushering in the wild and psychedelic visual cultural modes of the 1960s counterculture, which, despite some obvious dark sides and unpleasant developments, are largely associated with a sense of fun-loving freedom and liberation.

It is important to remember, then, that all drug images are not images of suffering. In fact, it seems to me that this distinction offers a clear entry point to thinking about the ways in which the *form* of the photographic image can be as significant in the construction of meaning as the subject: portraits—and, in particular, black-and-white portraits—lend themselves to capturing and communicating human conditions of suffering, and there is plainly something in the form that encourages an emotive response (empathetic or otherwise).

Drug scenes: *Reefer Madness* and visual drug culture

Leaving aside, for now, issues of portraiture and empathy (previously discussed in the introduction to this chapter and in Chapter 1, and also revisited briefly later in this chapter), let us consider the ways in which drugs interact with and populate contemporary globalized visual culture. Of course, 'drugs' is such a broad category as to be mostly useless, containing as it does everything from caffeine and nicotine to heroin and methamphetamine (and, of course, everything in between). I start, then, by briefly describing some significant and distinct trends and tendencies in visual engagement as they relate to specific drugs. There is, after all, a vast gulf of difference between the sorts of images most readily associated with marijuana smoking and those associated with intravenous drug injection, and any visually sensitive criminological effort should strive to disentangle the various meanings embedded in these images whenever possible.

In 1936, an American church group commissioned the production of a film warning of the dangers of marijuana use. The film, which was produced under the title *Tell Your Children* and later screened under a number of titles before finally becoming known as *Reefer Madness*, was quickly purchased by producer Dwain Esper, who had already had some success with other films that sought to exploit cultural fears relating to race and crime, and recut to appeal to audiences on the so-called 'exploitation circuit' of the late 1930s.

The film was a relative success in the context of its release, making it a popular attraction in exploitation cinemas until the mid-1950s, when developments in film technology—and the general audience's changing tastes and technical expectations—largely rendered films shot in the 1930s obsolete. *Reefer Madness* was largely forgotten until the 1970s, when it was rediscovered by the American counterculture that grew out of the 'hippy' era of the 1960s. This new counterculture was already heavily influenced by a host of cultural material that drew together drugs and the image: from author Ken Kesey's Merry Pranksters, with their use of wild and intense psychedelic and day-glo aesthetics, to the revolutionary socialist organization the Black Panther Party and its distinct mode of revolutionary art, discussed later in Chapter 7, the cultural stage was set for films like *Reefer Madness* to take on new life. In this particular instance, *Reefer Madness* was recontextualized as a cinematic document of puritanical hysteria (see generally Starks 2015).

What is most significant about *Reefer Madness* in the broad contours of the drugs–image–crime relation, though, is that it is a single document leveraged in service of distinct and competing agendas. Given life as a vivid warning about the horrors of marijuana, the film's vision rolled and bounced along the waves of American drug and cinema cultures until it came out on the other side a satirical skewering of marijuana prohibition. The story of *Reefer Madness* also reminds us that visual images are hugely important in the construction of crime and, perhaps, most intensely, drug crime. In its inversion, moreover, we also see the ways in which a single image or film might take on various meanings depending on a vast array of factors including context and framing.

The film also, like other moments in which drug crime enters the visual register, is illustrative of the ways in which race is implicated in and by drug images: in *Reefer Madness*, we see early glimpses of the ways in which the coming war on drugs—discussed in the context of its own distinct aesthetics and visuality later in this chapter—would be an affair that was endless, bloody, racialized, and intensely visual. The film's message is inescapably racist, and it cannot be viewed through any sensibly informed contemporary lens as anything other than a propaganda piece warning not so much of the supposed dangers of marijuana, but of a menace the film presents as vastly more terrifying: non-white humanity. This process of racialization through drug images has, of course, serious material implications, as policy and trends in enforcement and punishment follow public concerns, which are themselves easily and often manipulated, exploited, or otherwise conditioned and guided by the images that take hold of the social imagination.

Criminologist Stephen Wakeman (2014: 225) describes the processes by which popular mediated images constitute 'cultural paradigm[s] of drug policy debates', while reminding us, importantly, that mediated images can be 'recognized as sites where meaning is *contested and/or generated*' (2014: 226, emphasis added) rather than simply handed down from power. Here we can also again briefly return to Brown and Rafter's idea of a (visual) public criminology (see generally Brown and Rafter 2013; Rafter 2017; Brown 2020) as a parallel tendency to academic criminology, one that emerges from public notions and discourses and mediated knowledge about crime and harm. It is not a great leap from there, of course, to recognize that the distinct public criminology of drugs is one configured largely by mediated drug images.

Among the examples in which we see mediated images contesting and negotiating meaning, drug images most clearly illustrate the political, historical, and criminological flexibility of the visual. Once the mark of a dangerous countercultural formation, for example, the neon psychedelia of the 1960s and 1970s was, by the late 1990s, the de-facto aesthetic language of a legal American cannabis industry worth billions, and *Reefer Madness*, largely divorced by history from the incalculable human suffering attached to the political formations it both produced and reflected, was transformed into a quaint and charming relic of American racism and moral panic to watch—stoned—in a college dorm room. By the dawn of the new century, these same sorts of images would be entirely antiquated, the detritus of an earlier generation, replaced by the new sleek and ultramodern design language of legal cannabis, an aesthetic borrowed more or less wholesale from the world of tech. The transformation, over just a few short decades, of these sorts of drug images, illustrates perfectly the ways in which capitalism and capitalist realism, described in Chapter 2, are able to absorb, eventually, even those images that are perceived as challenging its logics. That shift, though, also illustrates one of the central concerns and points of a visual criminology: images are often criminologically potent, and their criminological relevance and meaning are generally matters of framing and of the ways in which the forces of history, political economy, and power act on and through them.

Drug images in a contemporary panic: crack and cocaine

Drug images generally reach the zenith of their criminological potency when they become attached or integral to the construction of a drug panic. Because drug panics are mediated affairs that are enacted in headlines and on screens, drug images are often the most potent player in their construction. Surveying the contemporary history of mediated drug panics, at least in the US context, the crack 'epidemic' of the 1980s and 1990s stands out for its role in intensifying the power and pervasiveness of (anti-)drug images.

In the last two decades of the 20th century, the streets of America's cities—most notably Los Angeles and New York, but also urban centers like Houston, Detroit, Atlanta, and Chicago—were reeling from the arrival of crack, a form of rock cocaine that could be easily smoked, was highly addictive, and relatively easy to produce in profitable quantities. Crack, of course, is widely used as something of a high-water mark, a point that marks a significant shift in institutions including policing, politics, drug culture, and media. Crack's arrival in the American city corresponded with the decline, already underway, of what was thought to be a relatively stable urban economy, a decline with its own origins in the war in Vietnam, the ongoing drug war, President Reagan's final decimation of an already weak social safety net, and the death of organized labor.

As the seismic forces of history shifted, crack emerged in and from the US mediascape as the perfect scapegoat to explain the carnage of an inner-city left reeling by the retreat and consolidation of capital and increasing criminalization. As with most good moral panics and anti-crime crusades, the mediated panic surrounding crack cocaine began with children. In the early 1980s, some American pediatricians and natal care specialists began to note certain health issues and outcomes including low birth weights, fever, and respiratory issues in newborns that had been exposed to cocaine *in utero*. By 1985, physicians and researchers were publishing headline-ready papers on the effects of cocaine on fetal development, with some—like the now-infamous 1985 study (Chasnoff et al 1985) of just 23 cocaine-addicted mothers that formed much of the foundation of the ensuing panic—garnering thousands of citations and dozens of media reports. This research was received with great delight by a mediascape clamoring for the most shocking story to sell to an audience increasingly captivated by crime stories, increasingly engaged in television news programming, and increasingly hungry for salacious images and easy explanations for the vastly complex and multivariate problems of the day.

By the late 1980s, news stories about so-called 'crack babies'—the callous name the media gave to the supposedly growing cohort of children born to crack-addicted mothers—were commonplace, occupying space in the headlines and airwaves of virtually every American media company. These stories highlighted or were accompanied by images of such children, images seemingly designed to pull at the heartstrings of their audience. News crews filmed segments in neonatal wards of urban hospitals, filling suburban screens with images of tiny babies in incubators, connected to tubes and machines and seemingly too fragile to possibly survive. These images, of course, were intensely racialized: 'crack babies' were an almost entirely non-white phenomenon, born only to the Black and Brown mothers of the inner city (never mind that rates of cocaine use were more or less equally distributed across race). These images joined other drug images of the time, though, in providing the visual evidence of the world that Reagan-era drug warriors had warned was just around the corner.

While the racialized nature of the crack baby panic is essential in giving it its visual potency, it is not the only problem with the myth: it was also almost entirely untrue. While it is, of course, the case that children were born with health issues related to cocaine exposure, the conclusions of media reports and their audiences—that this was an epidemic, that it was largely or entirely a problem of and for Black and Latino women, that babies were born addicted and in withdrawal, and most importantly that this all signaled some broader moral failure in urban America—were not at all supported by medical and public health research. As it turned out, most of the physiological effects (such as premature birth, low birth weight, and so on) experienced by children born to addicted mothers were explained as well by poverty as they were by addiction, and that these effects were largely consistent across a variety of drugs, some legal and some illicit, some 'white' and some 'Black' (for a thorough description of this and further analysis of the medical and political forces at play in the construction of the problem of 'crack babies', see Lyons and Rittner 1998: 316–17; see also Logan 1999). The 'crack baby', then, was largely a fiction, a racialized and mediated image constructed and leveraged in service of various agendas and ideologies (Sagatun-Edwards 1998).

The figure of the crack baby was not, of course, alone on the stage of crack images in 1980s and 1990s America. This era also saw the rise of the gangster rap industry, which would usher in a whole new mediascape, one deeply conditioned by the presence and prominence of crack. As pioneering musicians like Los Angeles' Ice-T and N.W.A., Houston's Geto Boys, and New York's Tim Dog crafted what would become a new crack-inflected paradigm for popular music in America, filmmakers like Mario Van Peebles, John Singleton, and Allen and Albert Hughes brought the city to the screen with gritty and violent films that foregrounded the effects of the crack era on Black life in America. Among the films made in this period, it is Van Peebles' *New Jack City* (1991) that would give the most prominence to crack as a visual artefact: its scenes of crack production carried out on a near-industrial scale in wildly public environments and its depiction of crack addicts as possessing a desperation that disqualifies them from being counted as human immediately became centerpieces in the genre, appearing later in an endless list of movies and television series, including the hugely influential Hughes brothers' film *Menace II Society* (1993). Of course, these images, which contributed so significantly to the racialization of crack, were simply added to a much broader body of images from cinema and news media that had already emerged at the center of the mediated 'anti-drug' campaigns of the 1980s and early 1990s.

Documentary photographers also contributed to the construction of the image of the crack addict and the effects of the drug's ascendance on a community. Just like photos made by Gordon Parks and Larry Clark and John Ranard and others working before her in the tradition of addiction portraiture, Brenda Ann Kenneally's images of crack addicts and the scenes of their daily lives told an audience hungry for suffering what it meant to be an addict. Shot in the 1990s and early 2000s in New York City, primarily in Brooklyn's Bushwick neighborhood, Kenneally's photos are very much in the tradition of Parks and Clark and others, and they largely adhere to the aesthetic conventions of the genre as established in Clark's early work: they are shot in black and white, often with stark contrast and balance, and they feature what we are to assume are 'raw' images of conditions unaffected by the camera's presence. While many of Clark's images are more traditional portraits, in which the subject has posed and in which the inclusion of symbolic and iconographic elements might be more plainly deliberate, Kenneally's photos rarely contravene a more journalistic or documentary mode. Instead, the position of the camera in her images feels largely defensive, the lens less a window into a world and more a barrier to an artist. This tendency—to assume that positioning within a documentary or journalistic tradition somehow frees the artist from whatever ethical restraints might otherwise exist—is often a focal point for criticism of this sort of addiction and drug photography, a criticism leveled at Kenneally by critics who have described her addiction images as evidence of an absent conscience (McNatt 2004).

It is not, of course—or, at the very least, *should* not be—the purview of visual criminology to deduce the intentions of artists or images. Neither should the aim of the tendency be to craft for itself a dogmatic framework of ethics to somehow govern the production and reception of images. It is, though, the responsibility of the visual criminologist to remain attentive to the critical weight of meaning, and to remain mindful of the role of the visual in constructing and maintaining the meanings that configure and make the world around us. At the specific sites in which drugs, the visual, and harm, crime, and justice intersect, it is essential that visually attuned criminology make important interventions into mediated drug panics such as that surrounding crack, which are sure to only further harm and delay compassion and justice.

Of all of the (actual or ostensible) anti-drug images to emerge from the crack era, perhaps none has the cultural endurance—or the ability to illustrate the ways in which drug images are contested—of the 'public service' and 'educational' images produced as part of the US war on drugs and the Just Say No campaigns of the 1980s. The pet project of American First Lady Nancy Reagan, the Just Say No campaign and its equivalents abroad were defining features of the mediated landscape of Western visual culture in the 1980s and 1990s. In the US, the most enduring images produced by these efforts are the often-derided television and print adverts that metaphorized a frying egg as a developing adolescent brain, urging audiences to consider the ramifications of emptying their skulls into a hot skillet. It wasn't just the United States dabbling in this sort of visual anti-drug campaigning, though; the UK did not have Nancy Reagan and sizzling eggs, but Just Say No was a memorable and popular campaign there, too, with a 1986 hit single to match: the creatively titled *Just Say No*, performed by the cast of the children's television program *Grange Hill*, which reached number five in the UK Singles Chart. Later, in the early 2000s, the UK showed up at the party with the Talk to Frank campaign, a home office initiative to warn young people and their guardians about the dangers of drugs. Proving again the ways in which the meanings of images and their reception is unfixed and contingent, these campaigns seem less likely to encourage young people to reconsider drug use, and more likely to encourage them to produce and disseminate and take in mocking and derisive reimaginings and remixes of anti-drug images; in the college dormitories of the early 21st century, the 'this is your brain on drugs' image of the sizzling egg is only likely to materialize in satire, as in a popular poster that revises the message to conclude not with drug-induced brain damage, but instead with a 'side of bacon' being added to the 'brain'.

The mockery of these campaigns is also not limited, to the glee of youth everywhere, to these sorts of visual memetic remixes, either; in the wake of their chart-topping hit *Just Say No*, the teen cast members of *Grange Hill* were invited to visit the US White House for a meeting with the First Lady of the US and of the Just Say No campaign, Nancy Reagan. In interviews following the visit, cast member Erkan Mustafa claimed to have smoked a joint at the White House, a rumor the actor only dispelled—while admitting to being the one to have started it in the first place—in an interview with *The Guardian* in 2016, on the 20th anniversary of the visit (Saner 2016).

Finally, it is important to note that racialized drug images have effects that extend far beyond the cultural production of silly adverts and awareness campaigns: these images condition, inform, and act on our social reactions to drug-related crime, harm, and panic. The most famous example of this, with significant criminological relevance, is in the disparities between sentencing guidelines for crack and powdered cocaine that governed drug prosecutions. A result of the US Anti-Drug Abuse Act 1986, which enjoyed bipartisan support and was signed into law by Ronald Reagan as a symbolic and legal lynchpin in his intensification of the war on drugs, the abuse act mandated a 100:1 disparity in sentencing between powder cocaine (generally seen to be a 'white' drug favored in suburbs and boardrooms) and rock cocaine—crack—(generally seen, as described earlier, as a 'Black' drug favored by the dangerous working classes of the inner cities). Under these mandates, a defendant convicted of possession of 500 grams of powder cocaine would receive a sentence of five years' incarceration without parole or probation, while only five grams of crack cocaine would receive the same sentence. This disparity, a direct result of the visual process of fabricating a racial difference between two forms of the same drug, is deeply implicated in the explosive growth of rates of incarceration in the US, particularly, of course, for young Black men convicted of non-violent drug offenses. While the Obama administration celebrated a victory in the passage of the Fair Sentencing Act in 2010—which was hailed as more or less addressing the major flaws in the 1986 Act—although that legislation merely reduced the disparity to 18:1 (Linnemann 2016: 214). The images and ways of seeing, then, that flow from racialized drug panics have deeply consequential material and political effects.

Drug images in a contemporary panic: meth images

It seems that with each new drug panic, each new epidemic of addiction, to use the lingua franca of media, comes a new wave of images. Opium, the salacious drug scourge of Edison's day, captivated the earliest audiences of moving pictures. The gangster Al Capone, the 'hillbilly' moonshiners of the American South and other cultural figures associated with the illegal production and distribution of liquor during Prohibition became the antiheros of American cinema and literature. Later, in the wake of the American war in Vietnam, gritty 'realist' images of suffering addicts and glossy and gauzy images of prospering dealers both populated the visual cultural landscape. While each trend has, it seems, its corresponding corpus of images, perhaps none is as powerful as that associated with methamphetamines, a broad category that covers a host of drugs—some illicit, some entirely legal—most usefully understood as speed.

Long used by everyone from truck and taxi drivers to fighter pilots and factory workers, meth, as it is most often known, is a powerful stimulant that can allow the user to stay awake and, to some degree, alert for hours on end. Although meth was certainly popular earlier both as a drug and as a site and subject of drug photography and cinema—it features prominently in Larry Clark's *Tulsa* photographs, discussed previously in this chapter, as well as films like *Easy Rider* (1969) and *Drugstore Cowboy* (1988)—it reached a new degree of visual power and prominence in the late 1990s, when astute viewers of the television series *Cops* (discussed later in Chapter 7) would have begun to notice more and more camera time going to so-called 'meth heads'. As the hysteria surrounding crack had largely evaporated as the horrifying images of that crisis were increasingly understood as mythic, America would again find itself in the throes of a mediated drug panic, this one focused on methamphetamine.

Like crack and heroin, the effects of long-term meth use, criminalization, and the poverty and lack of social support associated with addiction are often plainly visible in and on the body. The images of intravenous heroin users in Bourgois and Schonberg's (2009) *Righteous Dopefiend* share much of their aesthetic DNA with Clark's *Tulsa* photos of meth users, shot nearly four decades later. Schonberg's photos make more use of black, but like Clark he often shoots against the light, giving his photos the same burnt and blown-out look as Clark's. Both collections prominently feature the act of injection, and both artists are happy to let their lens linger on the needles, spoons, candles, and other material artefacts of intravenous drug use, as well as the sores, scabs, and other wounds of their subjects (which are, significantly, much less prominent in images of users of non-injected drugs like crack). In some ways, what sets these images apart from each other is everything but the human subjects: the settings and surroundings of Schonberg's photos signal a contemporary decay, while Clark's subjects populate a world that has not yet been entirely wrecked.

Meth images, while clearly implicating the same sort of bodily concerns as other drug images, move away from the established 'realist' image of the injection drug user; once-familiar scenes of predominately Black and Latino addicts are recast with white characters, urban settings are replaced by trailer parks and farmland and small towns, and needles give way to sores and missing teeth. Of course, just as the newly emerging image of meth recrafted the contemporary tropes of addiction photography—meth rapidly recoded race, place, class, gender, the somatic body, and more in the popular visual imagination—so too did it begin to shape police and policing (Linnemann 2013, 2016; Linnemann and Wall 2013; Linnemann et al 2013; Linnemann and Kurtz 2014).

Just as crack and cocaine before it, meth also quite literally took center stage in American media in a compelling but entirely fictive form. Most notably, meth was given life on the (small) screen in smash AMC hit *Breaking Bad* (2008), a wildly influential and popular series that chronicles the rise and fall of science teacher-cum-cancer patient-cum-meth kingpin Walter White. A number of scholars have offered visually attuned analyses of everything from the series' portrayal of gendered violence (Wakeman 2018) to its role in constructing Albuquerque, New Mexico (where the series is set) in the visual and social 'geographic imagination' (Cook and Ashutosh 2018).

Perhaps most significantly, though, are the ways in which *Breaking Bad* and other mediated and fictive visual cultural productions construct, guide, and justify police power and violence. Linnemann (2016) offers a thorough account of the power that emerges from the intersection of visual media and drugs, reminding us that images, with all of their cultural, political, and social strength and potency, are fundamental in the production and reproduction of police power.

Drugs, images, and empathy

Of the key points at which the visual intersects with crime, harm, and justice discussed in this book, none are as deeply implicated in the problem of the ethics of the image—a problem described in Chapter 2 here and much more thoroughly elsewhere (see generally Carrabine 2012; McClanahan 2017; Copes et al 2018a, 2018b)—as the drug images in this chapter. While I am generally reluctant to enter into an exhaustive or comprehensive discussion of the distinct ethics of each dimension of the visual discussed here, the ethical dimensions of addiction images mentioned previously are so evident and striking that they warrant at least some discussion. So, before concluding with a discussion of the role of images in the policing of drugs, let us briefly consider some of the distinct ethical issues embedded in images of addiction.

Across every dimension of the visual discussed earlier, there is a persistent and nagging concern surrounding the ethics—and ethical limitations—of images of human suffering so commonly tied to addiction. Artists and documentarians have long struggled with these sorts of representational issues; as previously described, images tell vivid stories, but it is often impossible to embed the sort of necessary contextual information into the visual. Keenly aware of this issue, former heroin addict and photographer Graham MacIndoe (2018) has described the ways in which 'pictures of addiction on their own can be misconstrued and misread'.

Artists and everyday documentarians, though, are obviously only one side of the interactive processes implicated in photography, which demands interaction between camera, photographer, subject, and audience. The ethical implications of photography—and, in particular portrait photography, with its intense focus on the subject, and even more particularly addiction portraiture and other forms of drug photography, with their tendency to train the lens on human decay and suffering—are vast, and for a visual criminology arrive most fiercely on the social terrain of drugs. As Jennifer Evans (2018: 3) notes, Walter Benjamin and Susan Sontag were both deeply suspicious and doubtful of 'photography's ethical potential'. These limitations are, perhaps, especially meaningful for visual criminologists, who are frequently already engaged with populations that, for one reason or another, are particularly at risk of exploitation.

For criminologists working at the intersection(s) of drugs and the visual—and, in particular, for those creating original photographic images in the field, and even more particularly photographs of people affected by addiction—there are deeply important ethical considerations to be made. Some of these are described and negotiated usefully by Heith Copes and colleagues (2019; see also 2018a, 2018b), who note the ways in which the presentation of images of addiction-affected subjects should always be accompanied by a thoughtful and careful textual contextualization. These authors understand the images produced in their research as constituting an important countervisuality, one opposed to the one-dimensional, reductive, and dehumanizing visuality established in addiction portraiture. While there are, then, obvious and obviously important ethical concerns surrounding visual modes like addiction portraiture and other forms of drug images, and while mitigating and negotiating those concerns should be among the top methodological priorities of a visual criminology of drugs, there is a relatively robust framework on which visual criminology might rely to produce and engage sensitively and justly with images of addiction and drugs.

Images and the war on drugs

Each of the dimensions of drug images discussed here ultimately coalesces into the vast corpus of images at the center of the US drug war, the most visible contemporary engine behind the spectacles of carceral and police power. While more thorough discussions of those two sites of power and the ways in which they are visually constituted and expressed can be found, respectively, in Chapters 6 and 7, it is important here to note that it is in police power where drug images find their most materially loaded affect.

The very 'conflicts' that fuel the growth of prisons and police power, then, are reliant and enacted largely on the very same images that produce and configure those same powers. Here visual criminology might briefly refine Debord's (2012: 11) assertion that 'the spectacle is capital to such a degree of accumulation that it becomes an image' in order to account for the multiplicity of images that constitute and reify power in the drug war. While images of suffering addicts might potentially compel some empathic response, any correspondence between that image and those of drug warrior police enacting violence is severed, and their relation obscured, in the swirling spectacle of the mediated drug wars.

The policing and punishment of drug crime is, of course, a relational event, and so it is useful to recall here Debord's point that the spectacle is more relational than it is corporeal. The distinct spectacle of the drug war is no different: it is a relational and real series of events, configured and accumulated with such visual intensity as to become spectacular.

Just as a racialized war on poor Black people was justified and supported by a mediated landscape of crack images, as discussed previously, the reconfiguration of the drug war to target white and rural poverty through the policing of meth relied entirely on the figure of the drug and its users in the social imagination. While figures like *New Jack City's* Pookie and photographs made by artists and documentarians like Arnade, discussed previously, swirl at the center of the war on crack fought in the inner cities of the 1980s, so too do images of a depraved Walter White in *Breaking Bad* and the wounded and exploited Faces of Meth swirl at the center of the war on meth fought in the rural landscapes of the 1990s and early 2000s (Linnemann and Wall 2013; Linnemann and Kurtz 2014; Linnemann 2016).

It seems as though the newest visual horizon to emerge in the war on drugs, at least in the US, is the image of the opioid crisis. Here, though, the relation between the visual and the criminogenic described previously through the example of cannabis is reversed: as legal prescription opioids like OxyContin and Percocet exploded into the underground drug economy in the 1990s and early 2000s, the drugs enjoyed a relatively legitimate and non-criminogenic image projected (and protected) by trademarks, brand names, lab certifications, marketing materials, prescriptions, and so on. Many users and sellers of these drugs, we know from research (Webster 2013; Kilmas et al 2019) and from listening to users themselves, find their introduction to the world of illicit opioids through legitimate initial prescriptions, and we might imagine that some concerns were no doubt allayed by the specter of safety and legitimacy projected on to these drugs by the forces of capital and marketing. As the opioid crisis has continued and shifted, though, the once polished and deeply institutionalized image of the entire global pharmaceutical industry—long derided for its seeming indifference to suffering and a host of historical scandals, but nevertheless an exceptionally valued juggernaut of industry and development—became tarnished, painted with the same brush applied previously to cocaine and heroin traffickers, marijuana users, and the racialized and dangerous classes.

One of the most intriguing dimensions of the opioid crisis' convergence with the visual is in the ways in which commercial images and the visuality of marketing have acted on the addiction crisis. In opioids, at least prior to the rise of off-lab analogs like fentanyl and other synthetic opioids around the mid-2010s, we find a crisis surrounding the illicit 'street' use of a drug with an image already firmly defined by marketing and commercial visuality. An interesting and noteworthy example here is the briefly scandalous moment in which the American media and public became aware of parody music videos produced by opioid manufacturers in the global pharmaceutical industry.

The most famous of these videos showed sales reps and even a vice president of sales at Insys, a pharmaceutical manufacturer, singing and rapping about Subsys, the company's highly addictive and deadly opioid spray, which is pharmacologically closely related to fentanyl, and was circulated among staff in order to drive corporate excitement, sales, and profits. These slickly commercial visual productions, it seems, were not adequately subaltern, sexy, or racialized to have the same sort of immediate ramifications as the images produced in earlier drug panics, and so the figure of the wealthy, white, besuited, male pharma executive escapes the scrutiny of our mediated anti-drug morality while the Black and Brown street dealer remains firmly in place as the human image of drug crime.

Conclusion

Drugs contribute vitally to the global visual cultures that configure the world in unique ways. Drug images, like all other images (and, perhaps, more than other images), are contested, their meanings shifting with changing applications of the forces of power, history, politics, political economy, and cultural production. In the history of drug images, we can locate some of the earliest origins of the racism and racialized and gendered framings that still so intensely condition criminological images today.

Drug images are also intensely mediated, with the worlds of drugs coming to life—and leading to death—in headlines, cinemas, television screens, literature, visual art, and the vast public imagination, and those mediated visions go on to inform and configure social, political, and cultural reactions, including policy. The intersection of drugs and the visual also, though, illustrates that the criminological image is always unfixed, a moving target, and also demonstrates the ways in which the dynamics of criminalization and cooption often wrestle for control over the meanings written into the images that emerge from a visual culture of drugs. Perhaps the most consistent meaning we can ascribe to drug images, like so many other categories, is that their meaning is largely determined by capital.

Finally, drug images are also among the most steadfastly powerful. In criminological terms at least, drug images do an immense amount of the image work of justice, and the specter of drugs haunts the public criminological imagination more resiliently than others. These images and visual cultures are deeply powerful actors, their mark evident in the most material manifestations of law, crime, harm, and justice in the game—that is, punishment and police, the final two substantive fields of a visual criminology described here in the following chapters.

6

Punishment, Prisons, and the Visual

Introduction

Like many of the other issues and sites taken up in this book—and, more generally, taken up by criminology—the ways and moments in which we *imagine* the prison are intensely configured by the ways and moments in which we *see* the prison; how we understand the concept of the prison is conditioned by how, where, when, and what we see when we look for or at the prison as a material space, as a building and as a location. The inverse, though, is also of course true: what we look at and for when we look for the prison in the vast landscapes of visual culture is conditioned by what we imagine the prison to be. Caleb Smith (2013: 167) cuts to the heart of this relation, noting that 'the penal state is operative in sites where we might not be accustomed to look for it'. It is necessary for a visual criminological exploration of punishment to think expansively about when and where we might render regimes of punishment visible, or to otherwise use images in order to wrestle meaning from punishment.

It is obviously essential, then, when thinking about the visual dimensions of punishment, that we not limit our analysis to prisons. Like police, described later in Chapter 7, the full form of punishment is first obscured by thinking solely of the prison. In the example of police, the problem arises from the limitations imposed by 'the', whereas in the case of punishment the limitation is imposed by 'prison'. It is important, then, to remain mindful of the vast apparatuses of punishment that extend beyond and outside of the confines of the prison.

Given the scope of tendencies implicated at the intersection of the visual with prisons and punishment—including everything from the material space of the prison to the virtual spaces of 'e-carceration' and other trends in non-custodial supervision, as well as the incalculably vast archive of images flowing from the social facts of the prison and punishment—it may be useful to think instead simply of a 'carceral culture' (that is, a culture entirely conditioned by a carceral regime and carceral political economy), a category that captures the full range of carceral possibilities. Michelle Brown (2009: 56) describes the ways in which this 'culture of punishment' is made and remade through the production and reproduction of penal spectators, also noting elsewhere (Brown 2014) that we are now firmly in a 'carceral age' or epoch. Schept (2013: 73), meanwhile, identifies what he calls a 'carceral habitus', the 'capacity' of the practice of mass incarceration to 'to structure individual and community dispositions'. We can also, then, think of the images produced by that culture, whether they be images explicitly *of* prisons and prisoners or images in which the carceral culture is made real or implicated through other settings or subjects, as simply 'carceral images'.

Because the prison is such a vast site—one that encompasses far more than is implied in the particular materiality of the word 'prison'—this chapter, like others in this book, reckons with the prison not only as a real material and cultural space and place (and also ideology and logic), but also as an imagined one. The prison and other sites of a carceral state, after all, only become material after first being imagined, and the reproduction of the carceral logic and regime rely on the co-reproduction of the images that justify and facilitate carceral power.

The visible prison: prison architecture

The fact of punishment that, to my mind, most immediately suggests the potential of a visual criminological tendency, is the prison. Because of its distinct materiality—prisons are, after all, far more concrete, quite literally, than many of the other topics that generally fall under the purview of criminological interest—the prison provides an opportunity for criminologists to think about spaces and places, categories that necessarily implicate the visual to some degree, and that are generally disregarded by criminology writ large.[1] While this chapter endeavors to be guided by a conceptualization of 'punishment' that allows it to extend beyond the prison in order to capture more of the essential dimensions of contemporary carcerality, we nevertheless begin with some brief ruminations on the physicality and materiality of the prison.

Among the facts of its materialism, it is the prison's architecture that is most immediately compelling visually. Carceral geographer Dominique Moran (2015: 13) notes that prison architecture is not given its due in criminology and the sociology of punishment, despite the design of carceral spaces playing a significant role in 'how the goals of a criminal justice are materially expressed'. Just as what we find when we go searching for the image of the prison is conditioned by what we expect the role, function, and effect of the prison to be, so too does the design of the prison space itself express whatever dominant perception of the prison built it. Prison design is especially implicated in a contemporary moment in which the materiality of prisons and jails is rapidly expanding, with new facilities constantly being constructed and plopped on to the landscape in order to meet the demands of mass incarceration and a penal state that increasingly fills in for a withered social safety net.

In some sense, the prison as a building must also be seen to exist, optically and materially, in order to be seen, imaginatively and socially, to punish: socio-political calls for punishment, as part of routine statecraft, can only be satisfied by the convincing appearance of a place in which punishment happens. This is certainly not to say that the prison always appears visibly; prisons and other material constructions of the carceral state are often and perhaps even increasingly *in*visible in both material and cultural spaces, a problem discussed more thoroughly later in this chapter. Rather, it is to note that the material construction of the prison happens at the command (real or assumed) of the social and political body, and so the language of its design reflects the broader visual language of a penal state and carceral culture. Moreover, the design of the prison or jail is significant, in that it is an opportunity for the state to craft and project its own image. It is little wonder, then, that many early prison designs favored the sorts of imposing gothic forms that we still most often associate with the prison as a cultural institution. Prisons, then, are in some ways the face of the state, and they are often shrouded in masks that project strength, security, and power (see generally Fiddler 2007).

Prison architecture today, of course, is more diverse than it was in the time of the 18th- and 19th-century social reformer Jeremy Bentham or even the 20th-century philosopher Michel Foucault. While there is no monolithic image of the contemporary prison, there are obvious and immediately familiar visual tropes surrounding the prison: as a material setting, we usually imagine that we know a prison when we see it. It is hard to imagine, for example, watching a film or television series set in a prison and wondering to yourself just what this place is. Of course, as noted and described earlier, what we see reflects what we are looking for and what we are expecting to find, and more importantly what is expected from the prison by the carceral culture that built it. The archetypical American prison—an aggressively grim place, built in the panoptic model and generally featuring remarkably degraded and dangerous environmental conditions and reflecting a design philosophy that most would understand as fundamentally indifferent or hostile to human comfort and health—reflects the distinct carceral culture of the US, in which an aggressively punitive culture of punishment and incarceration is deeply enmeshed in the political economy. In parts of

Europe like Scandinavia and other Nordic states, meanwhile, carceral cultures manifest themselves in prisons with an entirely different aesthetic vocabulary, one that emphasizes light, cleanliness, privacy, and social and individual health and that generally reflects a carceral culture that emphasizes rehabilitation over punishment.[2] While these distinctions may be ultimately only aesthetic—after all, while most would choose a Norwegian prison cell over an American one, far more would simply choose freedom—they do nevertheless illustrate some of the ways in which the visible form of the prison corresponds with dominant ideologies and logics of punishment. The relatively progressive penal regimes of Scandinavian Europe are also not the only settings in which we see changes in penal aesthetics. Punitively oriented carceral regimes like that of the US have also realized the discursive and symbolic value of penal settings that eschew the traditional aesthetics of the prison in favor of softer spatial carceral technologies like the 'justice campus' described by Schept (2015), which, of course, serve ultimately to conceal the realities of carceral space.

Criminologist Michael Fiddler (2007) has described that correspondence in the context of prison cinema, a category discussed more thoroughly later in this chapter. As Fiddler notes, though, the cinematic figure of the prison has largely arisen to supplant and replace the architectural figure of the prison. Describing this transition, Fiddler notes that it is in the representational image of the penal setting in film or television that we now find the 'interface between the public and the prison' (2007: 192). Whether in the material realness of the prison as a building or a geographic site, with all of the communicative power attendant to materiality, or in the representational unrealness of fictional cinema and television, the fact remains that the prison derives a great deal of its power from the forces of the visual.

The visual prison: panoptic design

Most directly, prison design illustrates the particular penal techniques and technologies of the day. Here the visual is again heavily implicated, not only in the fact of their architectural design, but also in the quotidian functionality of prisons, as so much of the space of the prison is designed with seeing in mind. Prisons are, after all, largely intended to facilitate constant surveillance, an aim with obvious visual implications. Bentham's panopticon—a concept constituting both a design goal and tendency and, more broadly, a system and philosophy of control—is, of course, foundational in the ways that prisons are designed, built, and imagined, and most carceral design is still done in its language (see generally Semple 1993). The panoptic ideal is embodied most clearly in the vision of a series of cells arranged around a central tower in such a manner that the cell's occupants can be seen at all times from the tower, while the tower's occupant remains invisible (see Figure 6.1). The panoptic prison design would, it seems, satisfy not only a carceral culture demanding the total surveillance of a criminal population, but also administrative and technocratic demands of the sort of carceral neoliberalism that configures most contemporary global political economy. The panoptic tendency, though, does not stop at the

Figure 6.1: Drawing of Bentham's panoptic prison design by Willey Reveley, 1791

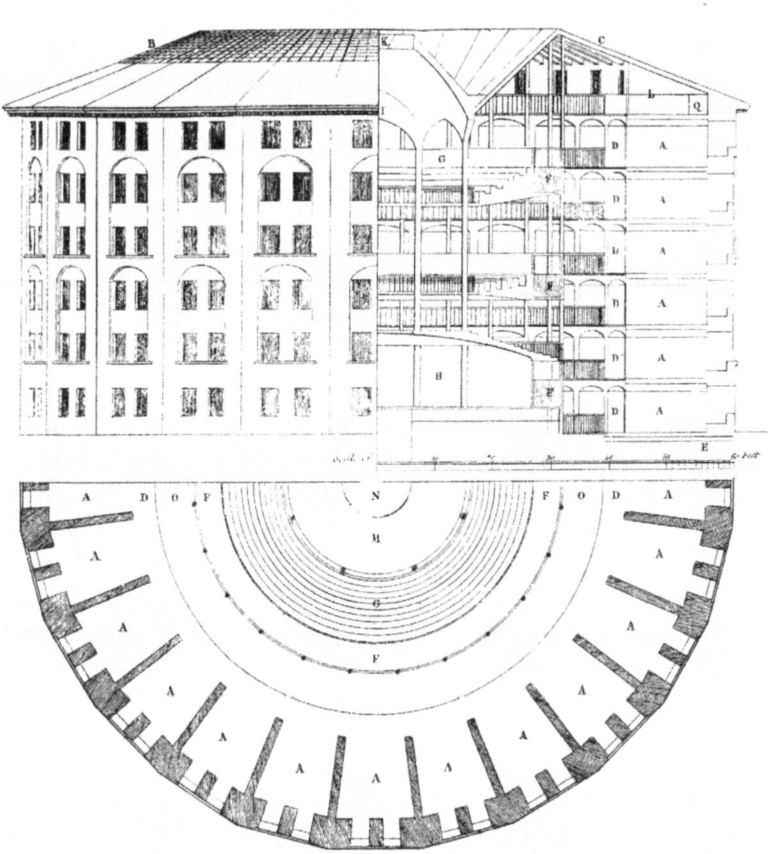

Note: The top half, a cross-section, illustrates the arrangement of cells alongside the outer ring so that they are visible from the central guard's tower, as illustrated in the lower half, which further underscores the elemental visuality of the panopticon with its resemblance to a diagram of a human eye.

Source: Courtesy of WikiMedia Commons.

architecture of the prison. Foucault, of course, famously reformulated the scope of Bentham's panopticon, insisting that it be understood not only as definite material space but also as an expression of political technology and power. For Foucault, the panoptic gaze was never limited to the purpose-built prison, but rather that it stretched across space and history, the central mode and tendency in disciplinary punishment, but also in the production and maintenance of power.

Seeing prisons

The images produced in and by a carceral culture correspond to the visible materiality of the penal regime: prisons and jails and the other material sites of punishment are material, and as such are (often, sometimes) visible. In some sense, these spaces are also among the most physical reminders of state power in the contemporary landscape, a material feature entirely necessary in the 'project of state building' (Gilmore 2002: 16) and criminal deterrence (Fiddler 2007: 192). Of course, then, it follows that in order to be maximally effective in statecraft, the carceral apparatus must, at least at times, be intensely visible, as discussed previously. Nowhere is that apparatus more immediately visible than in in its most familiar form, the prison, and so it is then little wonder that the prison so often looms over both the geographic landscapes of the material world and the conceptual and imagined landscapes of the worlds of visual culture.

Despite this looming, though, the penal state is also sometimes oddly occluded, hidden from view. Some of that diminished visibility, no doubt, has to do with the growth of the material penal apparatus: there are many, many more jails and prisons on the global landscape of 2020 than there were on that same landscape in 1960, and their ubiquity has reduced their remarkability. Some of that is also likely attributable to the various and significant ways in which the political and social body of advanced capitalist states is often encouraged by subtle social codes, cues, and norms to pay no mind—to not see, even only by the mind's eye—incarcerated people. Some of that diminished visibility is also, perhaps, part of a sort of fatigue, in which the image of the prison and all it entails becomes dull and old hat to audiences largely disinterested in the particular human drama and horror of incarceration. Finally, the reduced visibility of prisons is in no small part attributable, as Fiddler notes, to the ways in which modern prison design has abandoned the Gothic flourishes of the prison, with all of their foreboding communicative power and symbolism, in favor of a modernized 'empty', 'blank', and 'indistinct' design that, more or less, encourages us to look right past it precisely because it is too bland and meaningless to bother with, a perfect example of the logic of 'nothing to see here' that, as discussed throughout this book, is so elemental in the relation between power and seeing.

Although the particular materiality of the prison might not always come into view, at least in a contemporary world in which the visibility of a building called 'the prison' is no longer understood as totally necessary in order to maintain a diffuse sense of surveillance and potential punishment, it is nevertheless the case that distinct visible and material markers of the penal state exist all around us. In the US in particular, this materiality often emerges visibly in the presence of vast infrastructural networks, both formal and informal, that are tied to the carceral apparatus.

Filmmaker and author Brett Story captures some of those networks— as well as images that uncover and reveal both the visibility and invisibility of the prison—in her film *The Prison in Twelve Landscapes* (2016). The film, in many ways, is very much a 'criminological documentary' similar to work by David Redmon, previously described in Chapter 3, although Story forgoes the more narrative form of the mode in favor of a more abstracted approach. The film traces the outline of the prison in places where the prison is not, including on the buses that transport family members, often from major cities to the far-flung rural prisonscape, the stores that support the demand for supplies that can be reliably shipped to prisoners, and—perhaps most importantly—the sorts of everyday encounters with police and the criminal justice system that introduce the opportunity for incarceration. In each of the film's 12 vignettes, the prison is the elephant in the room: plainly present, yet plainly unseen (see Figure 6.2).

The tension between the visibility and invisibility of the penal state explored by Story also returns us to the quotation offered at the beginning of the chapter, from Caleb Smith (2013: 167), who reminds us that 'the penal state is operative in sites where we might not be accustomed to look for it'. One of the great strengths of Story's film—and, not coincidentally, one of the great strengths of visual criminology—is in thinking seriously about when and where to look, resisting the power of the carceral state to 'structure our very capacities to see' it (Schept 2014: 202). While the material sites of punishment and carcerality (the prisons, jails, and other buildings that constitute the material architecture of criminal justice) might be unremarkable to the point of unrecognizability or even entirely outside of our capacity to see, what we might think of as the material prisonscape extends infinitely beyond its boundaries.

Figure 6.2: Still from *The Prison in Twelve Landscapes*, directed by Brett Story, 2016

Note: For filmmaker Brett Story, the prison is visible in the landscapes of capitalist de-development that constitute the contemporary material carceral state, such as in this image of an Eastern Kentucky roadside.

Source: Photograph by Maya Bankovic, courtesy of Brett Story.

Carceral landscapes and penal invisibility

While prisons and other material locations of the carceral state often fulfill some of their purpose by looming in the visual, those same spaces are also often—and, perhaps, increasingly—occluded from view, as described earlier. In the US, in particular, the vast openness of material North American landscapes has lent itself usefully to the processes by which mass incarceration is hidden in plain sight. There are a number of drivers and explanations for what is commonly called the 'rural prison boom' (which we should modify slightly to include the parallel growth of rural jails), including the often desperate realities of rural economics in a post-industrial US (Huling 2002; King et al 2003), the ongoing construction of race and racialized criminal categories (Bonds 2006, 2009; Walker et al 2017), the need for new carceral spaces to fulfill the aims of the federal government (Norton and Kang-Brown 2020), and growing concentrations of labor power within the administration of carceral apparatus (Gilmore 2007), to name but a few.

The construction of material carceral spaces in secluded and/or rural landscapes serves, obviously, to reduce their social and material visibility. Taking up the supposed exceptionality of CIA 'black sites', Christopher Glazek (2012) argues that 'as far as the outside world is concerned, every American prison functions as a black site'. Tying the carceral landscapes of American mass imprisonment to the redacted and hidden landscapes of the global war on terror and its concomitant black sites, Glazek highlights, if not intentionally, the fundamental invisibility of carceral rurality. Dylan Rodriguez (2006: 10) similarly describes the visibility of CIA torture at Abu Ghraib as concealing, by way of its own hypervisibility, 'the intimate and proximate bodies … locally and intimately imprisoned' in domestic American prisons. Trevor Paglen (2010), like Glazek and Rodriguez, characterizes American prisons as 'blind spots' on the 'political and moral register of U.S. civil society and its resident establishment' (Rodriguez 2006: 10). Paglen underscores this point again in his observation that American prisons 'built since 1980 or so are way out in the middle of nowhere', noting that the 'physical isolation' of carceral rurality 'translates into a kind of invisibility' (quoted in Small 2015).

It is not just rural landscapes in which the material architectures of the penal state and carceral culture conceal themselves. In early 2015, British newspaper *The Guardian* reported on a complex of buildings in Chicago, Illinois, secretly managed by the Chicago Police Department (CPD) and used, as other reporting would go on to uncover, as a clandestine setting for the holding, interrogation, and torture of prisoners (see Taylor, 2015)—most often young Black men picked up in indiscriminate sweeps of 'hot spot' neighborhoods, but also criminal suspects in active investigations—whose whereabouts and carceral status (if they were in custody, where they were in custody, bail amounts, and so on) were concealed. Those taken to the complex, at Chicago's Homan Square in the city's bustling West Side, were renditioned, taken to a large secret police complex in the urban core of a major American city. The families, friends, and legal representatives of those taken to the facility had no way of knowing where they had gone, as being taken to the Homan facility did not produce any sort of record of detention or interrogation, or even any record of police contact at all. Many were held for days in the complex, which was designed as a warehouse, and only very rarely were detainees taken to the facility permitted to speak to their attorney (see generally Hudson 2015; McClanahan and Linnemann 2018). Of course, the material site of Homan Square is visible, and of course members of the public knew that people were taken there by police, but because there were no booking documents, or records of arrest or detention, and because detainees were generally kept 'off the books', prisoners in the facility were essentially rendered legally invisible.

While the program of rendition that the police ran out of the Homan Square facility went on for years, the site never attracted attention. It remained an active, secret police station, a small complex of large buildings in the middle of Chicago that, at any given moment, was occupied by hundreds of criminalized women and men who had been taken by police, disappeared into the vast architecture of the criminal justice system. Of course, for the facility to remain a secret—even an open secret—there had to be some efforts made to conceal it, and so the building obviously did not bear the marks of other police facilities, designed to affirm, not deny, the police installation. Like the invisibility of the prison, though, the concealment of sites like the CPD's facility at Homan Square requires a parallel disavowal, a willingness—even an eagerness—in the spectator to look away from and forget the spectacle. As Linnemann and Medley (2019) describe, while there are plainly evident ways in which the CPD facility can be understood as a 'black site' in the sense that it is an off-the-books location in which detainees can be held and tortured without any formal legal processing, to understand the Homan Square complex as a black site is to, even if unintentionally, imbue it with difference. As these authors note, though, the complex is really more emblematic of quotidian operations within US policing than it is of any exceptionality. In some sense, we can also understand the revelations and reporting surrounding Homan Square as the 'inoculating' image, to return to Barthes (1972), that inures the social body against the greater harm of some bigger evil, in this case the global carceral apparatus.

New carceral technologies

While the most spectacular and exceptional part of the story of Homan Square might ultimately be the relative invisibility of a large police installation, there are a number of trends that support criminologist Michael Fiddler's assertion that 'prison as the visual location of punishment is in retreat' (2007: 192). While Fiddler is right in noting that the prison is in retreat as the most visible location of the carceral state, this does not, to be clear, mean that the careceral tendency is in retreat alongside it. There are, of course, many explanations for this phenomenon, and much like the prison, the explanation you find is largely determined by the one you look for. While in certain contexts and by certain measures there have been modest reductions in rates of incarceration (see generally, for example, Ghandnoosh 2019), there has been a parallel increase in the rates of growth for non-penal and non-custodial carceral forms of criminal supervision (Patten 2016: 86; see generally Fitzgibbon et al 2017).

Among the tools and logics that have emerged to fill the void left by the retreat of the iconic and visually powerful prisons of yesteryear, it is electronic monitoring that seems to have the most contemporary salience: the retreat of the prison is accompanied by the rise of 'e-carceration', the conceptual shorthand for a system of technologies that facilitate the non-custodial carceral monitoring and supervision of offenders. In this category, James Kilgore—who describes e-carceration as 'the successor to mass incarceration, as we exchange prison cells for being confined in our own homes and communities' (2016)—notes, we should include not only the kinds of quasi-penal technology of the house-arrest ankle monitor, but also seemingly non-penal technologies like license plate readers, 'stingray' devices used by police to capture cellular data, facial recognition software, and the massive metadata databases that archive all of the information generated by the digitization of carcerality. The prison has, then, retreated, but the carceral tendency and impulse has not, as more and more offenders find themselves supervised by probation, parole, house arrest, registries, and electronic monitoring. Put simply, these new technologies only illustrate a strengthening of the penal state rather than some innovation away from it.

Seeing a culture of carcerality

The work of visualizing a carceral state, Brown (2013: 113) notes, most likely 'begins at the cinema'—like so many other material and cultural forces of contemporary life— where punishment animates narratives, characters, and settings. Here, Brown joins Fiddler (2007), who as previously noted describes the appearances of the prison in films and television series as the 'main interface' between the public and the material penal state. Like drug cinema and police cinema, discussed more thoroughly in Chapters 5 and 7, respectively, what we can imagine as prison cinema plays an absolutely crucial role in constructing and communicating the image of the carceral apparatus, and those images in turn condition and influence the forces of punishment beyond the cultural scripts of cinema.

Like other genre forms and modes, prison cinema has its own scripts, conventions, and 'cinematic vocabulary' (Brown 2009: 58). The scripts of the genre are instantly recognizable, the roles predetermined and rigidly fixed. From classics of American cinema like *Cool Hand Luke* (1967) and *American Me* (1992) to television series like *Oz* (1997) and *Prison Break* (2005), the prison and its inhabitants—inmate and guard alike—capture and captivate audiences on screens both big and small, with deeply familiar images of carceral environments and characters. Moreover, the modes and motifs of prison cinema, as with the police cinema discussed later in Chapter 7, have seeped into virtually all other genres (Brown 2009: 56), so that the figure of the prison looms somewhere in the history, margins, or foreground of every other cinematic genre configuration. In cinema, then, the logics that animate the carceral state do not need to be visible in the form of the prison to be known, or even to be seen: in a social imagination conditioned by a culture of punishment and an endless barrage of carceral images, punishment and the state apparatuses that facilitate and justify it are facts of life that exist independently of what we might see.

Carceral images certainly do not stop, though, at the cinema. Instead, they emerge with the same ubiquity in television, literature, music, news media, commercial, fine art and documentary photography, and virtually all other cultural products and productions. *Monopoly*, among the world's most beloved family board games, features jail. In television series like *Oz* and *Prison Break*, an image emerges of a carceral atmosphere that is wildly and unpredictably violent and brutal, while in series like *Arrested Development* (2003) and even *Orange is the New Black* (2013), carceral spaces are often little more than a stage on which human drama can play out largely unaffected by the carceral setting. Images that reflect a culture of carcerality may be images of the prison environment, but they may just as readily be images of the logics and ideology of the carceral state and its various material apparatuses. They may also, though, be the sorts of everyday images of crime and harm that justify and fuel the carceral state through their role in the construction of a carcerally expressed 'punitive sentiment' (Price 2005; Frost 2010; Ramirez 2013). In some sense, then, images that implicate crime also always co-implicate punishment (and also police, a fact of police images discussed thoroughly in Chapter 7). Similarly, Phil Carney (2017), describes the ways in which the image is essential in the performative dimensions of punishment, representation marshalled into service to satiate a public with a well-developed appetite for punishment and cruelty.

The prison has also been quite significant in the development and history of fine art, particularly Western art (fitting, of course, given the Western origins of hegemonic carceral logics). Carrabine (2019: 211) traces the ways in which the prison, in particular, has emerged in art, arguing that 'punishment has an art history' that can be studied in order to reveal 'indications of the obsession with torture and incarceration that comes increasingly to the fore in the last decades of the eighteenth century'. The prison figures as a prominent feature in the landscapes—a concept itself, Carrabine reminds us, that is 'a cultural practice' and 'a medium naturalising deep seated political agendas', just as photography and visual representation are—of fine art quite prominently. Carrabine describes its emergence in the works of 18th-century Roman painter Giambattista Piranesi, which Carrabine argues 'have had such a grim resonance on our own times'. That tendency is also evident in the centuries immediately preceding the rise of the carceral state, though, in work from important Western artists including Goya's *Interior de Cárcel* (1793–94), Rembrandt's *Saint Paul in Prison* (1627), and Michelangelo's *Prisoners* sculptures (1505–34).

Cultural invisibility

The type of selective invisibility enjoyed by the penal state and discussed here is a two-way process, one that also requires an audience of spectators willing to not see, or to *un*see, the various arms of the penal state. While the material redaction or concealment of the penal state by way of its siting 'out there' in the hinterlands is a geographic process, it is one that cannot undo the knowledge, in the social imagination, that carceral spaces are out there somewhere. For that, carceral culture relies on a psychogeographic (see generally Debord 2008; Self 2007) process of strategic ignorance and disavowal—described earlier in Chapter 2—by which the political body can wash its hands of the violence done in its name (McClanahan and Linnemann 2018; Linnemann and Medley 2019).

This disavowal of the material facts of the carceral environment and its residents, as noted earlier in this chapter, is, it seems, a deeply important dimension of the ability of carceral logics to guide social relations and to reproduce themselves. Within the dialectical tension of visibility and invisibility that conditions the prison and other material sites of the penal state, incarcerated people remain more or less invisible. This is not, of course, to say that we have no incarcerated cultural figures; our cultural imagination is chock-full of important and significant incarcerated people, both real and imagined. It is certainly true, then, that the charismatic or spectacular prisoner captures headlines and hearts; here I am thinking of popular anti-heroes like Britain's Michael Peterson, immortalized in cinema in the cult crime film *Bronson* (2008), or Australia's Mark Read, the inspiration for another popular crime story, *Chopper* (2000), or of deeply tragic and sympathetic victims of police malfeasance like Brendan Dassey of *Making a Murderer* (2015) or Damien Nichols of the famed 'West Memphis Three', a group of incarcerated young men whose gut-wrenching story of wrongful imprisonment inspired no less than four major documentary films. It is also true, though, that despite the power of these particular prisoner characters, the social and political body largely disavows knowledge of the existence of those incarcerated people who are not given their due 15 minutes, who are not humanized and made real by the camera. Story underscores this point, noting that 'prisons have disappeared and with them the people inside' (2017: 455). Here Story joins Fiddler (2007) in noting the ways in which the prison has vanished, while also highlighting that with it, so too have the lives lived inside disappeared. Finally, we might also understand the disappearance or retreat of the prison as emblematic of the 'character' of mass incarceration as 'a project of state impunity centered upon disappearance' (Brown 2014: 187).

Visual cultures in carceral spaces

Despite these processes, of course, prisoners whose existence is disavowed nevertheless exist. And, as would be expected, incarcerated populations create their own cultural formations. And like cultures outside of prison, those internal prison cultures are also often intensely visual.

Tattooing has been famously associated with prisons and prisoners for more than a century in the Western world. A key part of the aesthetic outcomes of the penal state, tattoos configure the 'look' of prisons and prisoners worldwide, real and imagined. While tattoos certainly serve the same purposes—that is, an expression of 'style'—in prisons as they do outside of prisons, in carceral contexts tattoos may also take on an enhanced evidentiary or communicative power. As markers of social affiliations, records of criminal involvement, and expressions of criminal toughness or hypermasculinity, prison tattoos are a key example of the ways in which prison cultures, like other cultures, produce unique visual cultural products. In the context of the prison, like in other contexts, tattoos also play an important role in the visual construction and expression of identity and the 'visual communication of moral careers' (Phelan and Hunt 1998). Finally, tattoos have also long been considered a marker of embodied criminality: even Lombroso, the father of criminological positivism and, as described earlier in this book, a key figure in the development of visual thinking in criminology, took a keen interest in the tattoos of his subjects in Turin, adding them into his cataloged archives of 'stigmata', physical markers of atavism (Morrison 2004: 68).

Other forms of visual art also form in and around sites of punishment. In prisons, for example, some prisoners paint, sculpt, illustrate, or otherwise produce visual art. Much of that art has also made its way beyond the walls of the prison: the aesthetics of distinctly carceral forms of tattooing discussed previously, for example, routinely adorn the bodies of people who have not been incarcerated, and distinct genres of visual art like those produced under the various umbrellas of lowrider, cholo, gang, and even neo-Nazi cultures are hugely popular, common, and influential outside of the confines of the prison. The ability to produce original images through illustration is also often employed as an economic lever in carceral settings, as customized items like cards, envelopes, and decorations can be exchanged for cash, goods, or protection.

While the examples offered here are all longstanding, we can also find new and emerging forms of visual production within prisons, jails, and other carceral settings. The global proliferation of cellular phones, and the inevitable processes by which they are smuggled into prisons, has allowed for the new phenomenon of prisoners producing their own videos. The moving images produced on prison cell phones generally show the day-to-day conditions of prison life, although there have been some more remarkable moments captured in this emergent genre, such as the preparation and execution of an escape in Southern California in January 2016. In that incident, three prisoners recorded themselves breaking out of the maximum-security unit of the Orange County Central Men's Jail in Santa Ana, California in a ten-minute-long video, complete with voiceover from one of the escapees and footage of the trio recorded over the nine days they remained free. In Bogotá, Colombia, meanwhile, in the midst of a massive carceral crisis in which the country's jails and prisons collapsed under the additional weight of the COVID-19 pandemic, inmates filmed riots in May 2020 that killed 23 in La Modelo, Bogotá's notoriously violent model prison. This prisoner-produced footage was sent to journalists at Vice News, and the network aired the video as part of a headline story on the conditions faced by prisoners in the country. The footage is deeply disorienting, precisely because it is evidence of a form of seeing the prison that we more or less assume to be impossible.

Counter-carceral images

We can imagine counter-carceral images like those discussed here, following Brown (2014: 178), as the images used 'by current and former prisoners, community members, artists, and scholars to counter mass incarceration', images that emerge from 'the centrality of social relationships' in the counter-carceral imaginary (2014: 186). Taking another approach, we might figure counter-carceral images, as Story does, as those that challenge the normalization of carceral logics by recasting or reframing the penal tendency as 'strange'.[3] This particular

Figure 6.3: *Missing: 2.3 Million Americans* **by Nicolas Lampert**

Note: This counter-carceral image uses a familiar and culturally powerful mode—the cardboard milk carton, which in the 1980s was famously used to circulate images of missing children—in order to challenge the logics and violence of the carceral state.

Source: Courtesy of Nicolas Lampert/www.justseeds.org

formulation also reminds us that counter-images are often made by recasting, contextualizing or recontextualizing, or combining existing images (see Figure 6.3), often through techniques like 'detournement' or the production of what Benjamin called 'dialectical images' (discussed more thoroughly in Chapters 2 and 4).

Counter-images can also, though, be produced as original images in the field. Judah Schept (2014) offers a robust example and account of this approach as well as an attendant analytical framework, noting that images play a deeply significant role in the ways in which we 'perceive the carceral state' and that the 'alternative vantages' offered by the counter-carceral image can improve the 'historical, spatial, and political acuity' of our perception of the carceral state. Working with a photographer, Schept engages in a 'counter-visual ethnography' in which, following Avery Gordon's (1997) sociological concern with the unseen worlds of social ghosts, images are produced that aim to counter dominant narratives surrounding mass incarceration by historicizing the carceral tendency within a continuum of racialized and patriarchal state violence. Counter-images in this framework 'must intervene in the visuality of mass incarceration … by revealing its historical contingencies, its instantiated and structured and yet precarious place in the landscape' (Schept 2014: 217).

There are also, though, ways in which an anti-carceral countervisuality is implicated outside of the relatively strict confines of 'the image'. If visuality, in Mirzoeff's formulation (discussed previously in Chapter 2), is the power to see—to claim the right to look—it is also the power to foresee, to imagine and condition the future. There is, then, a significant degree of visualization at the core of an abolitionist imaginary that formulates for itself an image of a world without prisons, against the visuality of carceral culture. That image, moreover, is expressed in the production of other images, what Story (2017) calls a corpus of 'abolition imagery'. For Story, these images (realized and produced, in her particular framework and practice, through documentary filmmaking) are a corrective or challenge to a stream of prison (documentary) cinema that often mistakes 'seeing' the abject failure and cruelty of the carceral state for 'dislodging' it. In this example, then, counter-carceral images are produced by a documentary practice that resists the tendencies of a 'humanizing prison cinema' (Story's examples of the genre include 2012's *The House I Live In* and 2010's *Mothers of Bedford*, both popular films that attracted significant audiences and critical attention). Quoting Michelle Brown, Story notes that humanizing prison films ultimately contribute to a 'visual iconography of social suffering' (2014: 176, quoted in Story 2017: 456), and that such an iconography has little utility other than to reproduce the same racialized logics of carceral violence that they ostensibly seek to resist.

Meaningfully resisting those logics, working to unsettle or dislodge the prison and carceral logics, and reasserting that incarceration and punishment are social processes that have serious effects on the lives of criminalized and marginalized individuals, groups, and populations requires the production of counter-carceral images and narratives that can challenge the prison's place as a 'key ingredient of our common sense' (Davis 2003: 18, quoted in Schept 2014: 203). In the visionary abolitionist imaginary, the carceral common sense, carceral habitus, and culture of carcerality—all, more or less, various ways of expressing the sense that every corner of our social and political imagination is captivated and colonized by a carceral tendency—are challenged by the demand to imagine and envision something else.

Finally, we might consider that the abolitionist imagination is the only possible countervisuality of punishment. If, it stands to reason, the prison and the carceral state are illustrative of visuality, then only abolition offers a comprehensive *counter*visuality. As Schept describes, the carceral habitus structures not only 'individual and community dispositions' favorable to mass incarceration, but also the 'oppositional politics' of 'people and communities who purport to reject it' (2013: 73). Measures like prison reform, then, reflect the tendency of a political imagination captivated by the visuality of a culture of carcerality. Only through the antipodal opposition of abolition is a truly countervisual image realized.

Conclusion

As this chapter has demonstrated, the world of punishment is a visual one. Criminologists and other sociologists and social scientists have reckoned with this in a number of ways, including work that considers prison design and architecture (Fiddler 2007; Jewkes and Johnston 2007; Jewkes and Moran 2017; Jewkes 2018), the cinematic power of the prison (Fiddler 2007), and visual arts and expression in prisons (Bernstein 2010; Taylor et al 2010; Earle 2018). Moving forward, visual criminologists might further explore the ways in which the image and punishment are relationally bound. Because prisons are such material things—objects, really—there is an especially crucial need for a visual criminology of punishment to heed the call made by Alison Young, discussed previously in Chapter 1, to move criminological engagement with the visual from 'object to encounter'; a visual criminology of punishment, in other words, would do well to resist the urge to translate the materiality of prisons into window dressing. Rather, a visual criminology of punishment and prisons could mine the vast visual archives of a largely globalized carceral culture for some grains of insight into why, how, who, and where we punish—and, for that matter, what it means to incarcerate and monitor and surveil the social body—insights that are likely already embedded somewhere in some carceral image or another, awaiting their revelation.

Such a visual criminology of prisons and punishment might also turn its gaze, though, away from the object-site of the prison and towards the subject-site of the lives lived under the custody or supervision of the carceral state. As this chapter has described, prisons and other penal environments are in many ways constitutive of their own distinct visual ecosystems, producing their own unique images, visual cultures, aesthetic forms, and visualities. Visual criminologists might, then, also find that these distinct registers hold new insights into the questions of punishment and incarceration. Here, visual criminology may find a natural ally, also, in the emergent 'narrative criminology' (Presser and Sandberg 2015; Fleetwood et al 2019) that seeks to uncover and analyze the ways in which stories and narratives influence social relations including harm, crime, and punishment.

Finally, let us return to the quotation offered at the outset of this chapter: 'the penal state is operative in sites where we might not be accustomed to look for it' (Smith 2013: 167). Recalling that we seek carceral culture where we expect to find it (jails, prisons), and that we often only recognize it when we have a clear idea of what we are looking for (jails, prisons), a visual criminology of punishment may be well served by decentering the material spaces of incarceration in order to better reckon with punishment as a relational force that is both constitutive and illustrative of ideology. The figure of the prison, after all, is also always lurking in the background of an image of police (discussed in the next chapter) and vice versa. By taking seriously all of the images produced by a culture of carcerality and punishment and the distinct and powerful visuality that animates those images, a visual criminology might more comprehensively make sense and meaning of trends and tendencies in punishment and incarceration.

Police and the Visual

Introduction

If prisons are routinely occluded as described in the previous chapter, then police is a power that suffers the opposite condition: the visibility of police is markedly high, with police images occupying a fantastic amount of space across visual culture, a condition that has led police to be described as 'by far the most visible of all criminal justice institutions' (Chermak and Weiss 2005: 502). The relation between police and the visual, though, reaches far beyond the binary condition of visibility or invisibility; police power is elementally connected to the visual image, and the moments of interaction between police power and the image are incalculably vast, both historically and in contemporary contexts. In this chapter, I understand police power as largely imagined, expressed, materialized, reified, and resisted through processes that are, at least in part, theatrical, melodramatic, dramatological and, above all, visual.

This is what Jean and John Comaroff (2004) describe as the 'theatrics of policing',[1] and it is largely the visual artefacts of those theatrics that I mine in this chapter for insights into the relation between police and the image. Even a fleeting glance, however, at the contemporary visual landscape will quickly overwhelm the attuned viewer with images of and from police; our visual worlds are, it seems, crawling with cops, their fingerprints smudging and distorting nearly every image. This chapter, then, describes only the broad contours of that relation. From 'Wanted!' posters and early efforts at biological criminology to the growing corpus of video images of police killings, this chapter describes the development of criminological analysis of the police–image relation and endeavors to uncover some of the myriad ways in which the image and the police always implicate one another.

Images of police

To begin thinking about the relational ties that bind police and the image, we might simply note the vast significance of the camera and other mechanical imaging technologies in the development of police power. This relation has been noted and described in length elsewhere, and at some length elsewhere in this book, and so I simply note, following Jonathan Finn, that the camera's historical position is as 'a panoptic technology used in the surveillance of targeted populations and as a tool in a more abstract project of regulating and training an aggregate social body' (2009: 6). The former of these indicates the police, in the sense of an identified material institution of individuals, while the latter highlights the centrality of the camera to the parallel development of police power and police logics. Here I refer less to the amorphous catch-all framework of 'law and order' and more to a specific type of administrative, executive, and prerogative power mandated to identify and eradicate, always coercively and often with direct physical violence, perceived and real 'threats' to the larger abstract order of private property. The logic of police, then, is a logic of virtually unlimited discretionary power to maintain a highly unequal status quo. We should also start by establishing a distinction, within the broader theatrics of police, between images of police and police images.[2] The former category, of course, is intended to capture the complete scope of images of police. Images in this category are not bound by their cultural or affective meaning, or by any qualities or conditions of composition, mode, or production, but only by their subjects: police. This condition, though, is only deceptively simple. Were this category of images only understood by the presence of uniformed (or otherwise immediately identifiable) cops, it would fail to capture the full scope of police. As several efforts to theorize police have affirmed (see generally: Neocleous 2000, 2014; Wall 2016; Correia and Wall 2018), police is most accurately and comprehensively understood as a powerful architecture of logics and tendencies. This is not a corpus of images of simply *the police*, but a body of images of *police*, a logic and power every bit as evident in an image of a CCTV camera as it is in an image of a cop.

The cop—in uniform or out—is still the star of the police drama and, in fact, of a staggering amount of non-police drama. Police characters permeate nearly every corner of visual media. This amounts to an essential dimension of what we can imagine as police 'image work' (Lee and McGovern 2013; see also Mawby 2001; Russell 2017), a set of processes by which police performs its various tasks—including the production of consent to be policed, the production of a pro-social image of the police, and the production and reproduction of social order—through the visual. Often, the image work we encounter at the intersection of police and visual culture is part of the processes of pacification (Rigakos 2011, 2016; Neocleous et al 2013; Wall et al 2017). Police image work is, it would seem, an increasingly powerful and elemental dimension of police power, as the force and ubiquity with which police exist in contemporary visual media make clear.

Police and media

Even without adopting the critical definition offered previously, the scope and scale of the global and historical portfolio of images of police are staggering. If we pause to consider the prominence of police in the images we routinely encounter, the weight of this archive quickly becomes clear. Across popular culture and media, cops are common specters, and the police logic a nearly constant presence, a condition I return to later in this chapter.

Christopher Wilson (2000) makes clear the extent to which police power has seeped into—or, perhaps, out of—the entire, vast field of cultural products and production, describing its representation in media as lending to police a 'remarkably high degree of cultural *visibility*' (2, emphasis added), a condition affirmed by even the most cursory glance at virtually any modern visual media. From the bloody drama of Doc Holliday and Wyatt Earp at the OK Corral dramatized in *Tombstone* (1993) to the slapstick procedural comedy of *Brooklyn Nine-Nine* (2013), police power largely comes to life in the pages of our novels, on the stages and screens of our theaters and cinemas, in the photographer's viewfinder and, ultimately, in our very imaginations.

As Yvonne Jewkes and Travis Linnemann (2017: 158) describe, police logics are reproduced, and the public fear of crime and attendant reliance on police affirmed, by a decades-long tendency in popular media to favor the pro-police images described by Wilson. From the fictional Mayberry in the television sitcom *The Andy Griffith Show* (1960–68) to David Simon's all too real Baltimore in the hard-hitting series *The Wire* (2002–08), popular media and popular cultural productions obsessively populate the visual landscape with cops. Indeed, Jewkes and Linnemann argue, shows like *Dragnet*, the long-running series about a fictional squad of detectives in the Los Angeles Police Department (LAPD), can be usefully and accurately understood as what amounts to conscious pro-police propaganda (2017: 159–60).

Even more directly, we could consider the vision of police presented by *Cops* (1989), the American television staple that for 32 seasons featured 'raw' footage of everyday policing and later, its contemporary, *Live PD* (2016), which followed the same format but added the unpredictability of live broadcasting. Both shows, of course, reduced (or, more accurately, elevated) police and policing to only its most visually compelling and morally and politically defensible dimensions.

In both series, the audience rides shotgun in the squad car, eschewing the comparatively hokey naivety of police drama in favor of the gritty *vérité* action of police reality. Both series, of course, present an image of police that was tightly managed; when scraps of narrative do emerge from the fog of action that conditions both shows, police are always firmly and positively protagonistic. Both series also, though, found themselves unceremoniously cancelled (in every possible sense) in early 2020 as the American audiences that made the shows so successful to begin with began to reject police violence cast as entertainment. Both shows, though, and the aesthetic form they have been so foundational in constructing, are testaments to the power and perniciousness of the police tendency to produce and reproduce police power through (among other things, of course) the image.

The thin blue line and images of a culture of police

The tendency described here is again made clear in the relatively recent rise of a new visual (and, in fact, material) economy of police images— a broad field discussed more thoroughly later in this chapter—that have coalesced, generally, around the 'thin blue line', a centerpiece of police ideology that Tyler Wall (2019) describes as functioning within the police imaginary as the line between 'civilization and savagery'. Visual artefacts of the thin blue line ideology now permeate nearly every corner of the visual register, with bumper stickers, clothing, signs, and an endless range of other consumable material products nearing ubiquity.

Most recently, the new visual economy of the thin blue line has been augmented by the inclusion of what is colloquially known as the 'Punisher skull', a stylized and flattened illustration of a human skull that is reminiscent, by design, of the symbol worn by a comic book character, Marvel Comics' *The Punisher*, who uses extreme violence (and importantly, unlike most other inhabitants of the various comic book universes, consumer grade firearms) against street criminals. American police, though, have eagerly adopted the iconography of the *Punisher* skull, and it now routinely appears in and on a truly staggering array of consumable products, from patches that can be sewn on to police uniforms to actual police cars, produced by a culture of police (see Figures 7.1 and 7.2 for distinctly racialized and violent examples of aggressive police logics). This sort of imagery is also, of course, an elemental part of police image work, in that it constructs an image of police as strong, the producers and upholders of equitable public order and social relation.

Figure 7.1: Blue Lives Matter graphic on a police cruiser

Source: Courtesy of Edward Vasquez/Alamy Stock Photo.

Figure 7.2: Punisher skull iconography reproduced as a knit patch marketed to police and their supporters, 2020

Source: Photo by the author.

Moreover, these notably and intentionally aggressive displays of police power and visuality indicate that police control over the visual image and its reception is, in fact, significant. Even in the midst of the international anti-police (or, at least, police-skeptical) protest movement sparked by the highly visible police killings of George Floyd, Breonna Taylor, and others in the US, police power appears to remain committed to employing a range of iconographic imagery in order to establish itself as courageous, brave, just, and fair, or, when more advantageous, capable or even happily anticipatory of incredible and deadly violence. The thin blue line and related visual expressions of police power, like the beloved-yet-feared beat cops and detectives of the silver screen, are an important part of the relation between police and the visual and the contemporary image work of police power.

These dramatic, theatrical, and fantasy-laden public expressions of thin blue line ideology and potential violence are just one of police's more dramaturgical expression of police power and logic. Another important and theatrical site of police image work and symbolic policing is what Linnemann (2017b: 58) describes as the 'visual economies of seizure, accumulation and trophy' that animate the police practice of the trophy shot, in which images are produced that show off police seizures of property (most recognizably drugs and guns, but also and increasingly often real estate, vehicles, and other material goods) or human quarry. These images contribute to a broader visual economy of police images, one that produces, reproduces, and circulates the images necessary to produce consent among the subjects of police power, and are ultimately an 'unvarnished representation' of police power.

Following Linnemann, we can read the police trophy shot genre as that 'unvarnished representation' of the power,[3] will, and mandate of police to deploy violence—symbolic, real, potential, and realized—in the production of order and the defense of capital. There is also, though, an opportunity to return to the ways in which, for Debord, the spectacle is constituted and brought into being and representation by capital, a condition shared by police, which is also constituted and necessitated by capital. As Linnemann (2017a: 70) puts it, the police trophy shot is 'a visual representation of capital accumulated at the point of a gun'.

Rodney King, police, and the camera

Police, of course, do not only produce and reify images, and real-world cops often find themselves the subjects of real-world visual accounts of police. Perhaps no such account of police is more salient in the contemporary moment and in contemporary history than the images of five policemen beating and tasing detained motorist Rodney King on the side of a Los Angeles highway, images captured in 1991 by the home video camera of George Holliday. Although the requisite media infrastructure for virality, as we would understand it in a contemporary frame, did not yet exist—there was, after all, no YouTube, no Twitter, and no other digital social media in 1991—Holliday's tape was seen by a staggering proportion of the public, effectively doing whatever the 1991 equivalent of 'going viral' was. Although similar videos would coalesce, over the following decades, into a macabre and ever-expanding canon of 'police cinema *vérité*'—a genre formation discussed more thoroughly later in this chapter—at the time there was a sense that the footage was new or somehow revelatory to a national audience that had, largely, successfully disavowed police violence in the two-and-a-half decades since the end of the civil rights movement.

Suddenly, though, the Holliday tape thrust the lived reality of policed subjectivity known to non-white communities and other members of Los Angeles' dangerous classes into the forefront. This is not to imply, though, that the footage found an easy audience; it was first broadcast, after over eight days of Holliday's efforts to find a local television news outlet willing to air the footage, by local MGM news affiliate KTLA. The initial broadcast, though, showed only nine seconds of the video, which totaled over nine minutes in length and captured no less than 56 individual blows delivered to King by the police. The portion aired was out of focus, and taken from early in the video, before King was entirely unable to move. In the segment that KTLA initially aired, King is seen trying to stand, although he is quickly slammed to the pavement by a cop. Four police officers were eventually charged with assault following more widespread and national dissemination of the footage. When the jury convened in the trial voted to acquit three of the officers (failing to reach a verdict in the case of the fourth)—the April 1992 decision that would spark the Los Angeles uprising and would see the city consumed with violence, much of it flowing forth from the LAPD, for six days and seven nights—the jury members would cite the initially aired portion of video as essential in their decision. To hear the jury's interpretation of the images, those nine seconds conclusively showed an enraged King attempting to fight off the cops circled around him.

The outcome of the King trial illustrates, with remarkable clarity, the ways in which the visual record is far from objective, the image far from unquestionable evidence. As Dorothy Bailey, the foreman in the criminal trial against King's police attackers, would recount after the trial's conclusion, she had 'assumed that the videotape showed everything that had happened', and 'was amazed to discover how much more of it existed than had been shown on television' (Almond et al 2017). Even in the case of what is—or, perhaps, was—the most widely viewed visual record of police violence in American history, a record that shows a man beaten quite nearly to death by police fists and batons, the footage was not enough to hold police to account. As Bailey describes, in fact, the defense in the trial did not even have to discredit or disavow the video, but rather only had to embrace it not as a record of police violence, but as a record of 'by the book' and acceptable police behavior. Of course, we know that 'the book' that police follow when they act 'by the book' is itself an instructional document of remarkable violence. It was nevertheless that same book that the police imagination—the culture of police in which we all live—mobilized in justifying King's beating. Put simply, the visual document of the beating became the exonerating document in the trial of the policemen.

In the decades since the beating of King and the uprisings that erupted in the wake of his attackers' acquittal, similar images of police violence have become far more ubiquitous, largely as a result of technological developments in consumer electronics: by the early 2000s, millions of citizens found themselves armed with tools like mobile phones and digital cameras, capable of documenting and communicating the violence of police. These conditions and their effects are described more thoroughly later in this chapter, and so here I simply note that the video of the King beating marks the start of a new era in policing, one in which police ideology and actors must respond to and manage a 'new visibility' (Goldsmith 2010; see also Thompson 2005) in which there are new challenges to police image work, visuality, and power.

Police images, culture, and visuality

The relationship between police and the image, of course, does not start and finish with the production of images *of* police. Police logic and the image, in fact, have always been inextricably and intimately entangled. The corpus of 'police images', as distinct from the corpus of images of police discussed earlier, is constituted by images made by police (or in direct service of the police logic). In this canon, we might find visual products like 'Wanted!' posters, and so on. This body of images, then, is set apart from the previously discussed images of police in part by what we might assume the intention of the image to be. After all, as discussed in Chapter 2 and throughout this book, images always bear the marks of intent (generally of either the producer or promulgator of the image itself). In the case of police images, we can understand that intent as simply reflective of what we can imagine as a police subjectivity. Put more simply, police images can be thought of as simply images produced by police or those images that police want us to see. We can also, following Linnemann (2017b: 243–4), note that police images can either be 'policing's controlled or approved image' or an unapproved, uncontrolled image that exists beyond the censorial and delegitimating power of police approval.

There is also at times a tendency to imagine that images produced by police and police images flow forth from a site of cultural production somehow distinct from others. In this formulation, which is essential and elemental in the development of criminological and sociological knowledge of police, police constitutes a subculture, one with its own rules and regulations that exist outside of the scope of formal institutional rules as well as dominant social norms. As Steve Herbert (1998: 343) describes it, this view holds that police are a 'social group differentiated from the general public', and as a result of that difference, the cultural artefacts (including images) produced by police are the products of a distinct subculture of policing. This conceptualization of police, though, misses what seems to me an essential point: there is no reason to point to a distinct and discrete 'police (sub)culture' because all global Western capitalist culture is a culture of police. As Mark Neocleous (2000; see also Wall 2019) and others have described, the construction of capitalist 'civilization' relied and relies on the material and symbolic power of police to fabricate, maintain, and reproduce order. What I mean here is that to imagine a distinct police subculture is to ignore that the logics and figure of police always already infect all cultural production. In *every* image of and from the cultures of global Western capitalism, the figure of police is lurking.

This ubiquity, paradoxically, has also produced a visual register in which the presence of police is so suffocatingly constant that even its absence becomes noteworthy, and so police looms, even if only spectrally, always. It seems necessary to insist that the role of police power in configuring contemporary culture be unobscured. Several scholars have, over the decades, gestured towards the notion—derived originally from the demand made in 1968 by the French Situationists that the youth in revolt 'kill the cops in their heads' (Boal and Epstein 1990; Plant 2002: 179; Jovanović 2004)—that there is a 'cop inside the head'[4] of each of us, and what I suggest here is that even when we encounter images seemingly free of police, our interpretive processes are inflected by the cops in our heads. All images, then, are in some

119

sense police images: every image of white patriarchy, capital, violence, or power is also an image of police.

Police images: wanted posters and mugshots

This is not to say, of course, that there are not some images that are *more* police images than others. Across the range of police images, perhaps none is more immediately recognized and recognizable—in terms of both its aesthetic mode and its cultural meaning—than the 'Wanted!' poster. Rachel Hall (2009) attends to the history of this variety of police image, which emerged in early 20th-century America, noting that the posters replaced previous iterations of the same sort of image that prioritized the reward offered over the social need for the arrest of the featured criminal. Wanted! posters, of course, generally used custodial images like mugshots and other similar forms of illustrative carceral documentation in their portrayal of their bounty. Mugshots are also, it is worth noting, at the core of the relation between criminology, the photographic image, and police and carceral power; the practice began more or less with the advent of photography, and was, by the late 1800s, standardized by French criminologist and police researcher and reformer Alphonse Bertillon[5] (Farebrother and Champkin 2014). While mugshots, as distinctly criminal images, have a very evident aesthetic form and mode—owing, of course, to Bertillon's efforts at standardization—describing and analyzing those forms does little to help us to use the image in order to properly theorize police power. Instead, we might imagine mugshots not as evidence of a distinct aesthetic form, but as evidence of a logic, one which insists that individual criminality can be constructed and communicated through the image, that the dangerous class bears marks which the camera may render visible. Following the logic, not the form, in turn allows us to understand a diverse array of images as performing the same essential function as the formal mugshot, whether those images appear in an early Wanted! poster or in a contemporary 'mugshot magazine', social media feed, or news broadcast.

As I have already argued—and as any student of either discipline already knows—photography and law are inextricably bound together. This relation is made most clear, perhaps, in the ways in which mugshots and their attendant Wanted! posters function as visual objects that by design communicate, achieve, and reify the aims of police power. Alan Sekula, in *The Body and the Archive* (1986), describes the development of the mugshot (and informal practices of photographing the faces and bodies of prisoners and police captives) as entirely entangled with the parallel use of photography in penal institutions and police stations in order to construct the archives of deviant and criminal images in use, at the time, by burgeoning phrenologically and physiognomically minded criminologists and penal reformers.[6] What matters most in this complex and entangled history, for the purposes of this chapter, is that mugshots (and other images produced in the mode and style of mugshots) are absolutely essential in the ways that power and capital have constructed the visual and material figure of the criminal, the ways in which that figure is always racialized, classed, and gendered within the elementally patriarchal system of police order, and, thus, the ways in which the image of the criminal, embodied in the historic mugshot, contains all of the violent logics of power, capital, and police.

Similar images produced in service to these same logics also, of course, populate more contemporary visual registers. Here we can consider the trend, in the US, of small-circulation print periodicals that curate and publish—usually on weekly or bi-weekly schedules—newspaper-styled collections of police mugshots. These publications and the aesthetic mode they establish have quickly become ubiquitous components of the spectacle of the American justice system. Indeed, as Finn notes, 'The police mugshot has become an icon in contemporary visual culture' (2009: 36). Wanted! posters, mugshots, and other examples of what Paul Lashmar (2014: 57) calls a 'police photograph' are not, however, banal or bereft of meaning and power. Rather, as Lashmar describes, these images have meaning deeply encoded into their mode and composition, meanings that coalesce around the presumable guilt of the subject for the express purposes of shame and humiliation. Indeed, as the psychoanalyst Jacques Lacan argued, the very creation by the state of an archive of images of supposed criminal offenders prefigures the likelihood of reoffense (see generally Bond 2012).

Mugshots, like basically every other mode or form that emerges from the intersection of justice, crime, harm and the visual discussed throughout this book, are also intensely gendered and racialized. Mugshots, of course, also engender and encourage certain affective responses, and those responses routinely reflect and reify dominant cultural narratives surrounding race, class, and gender. As Danielle Dirks and colleagues describe, mugshot magazines and other public displays of images in that mode often do more than establish the guilt of their subjects: they also provide a social stage for the expression of racist, classist, and sexist logics and sentiments (Dirks et al 2015: 170). Hall, in her history of the outlaw poster, notes the ways in which Wanted! posters grew out of a popular tendency, in the 19th century, to use forms and modes similar to the as-yet-to-be-developed outlaw poster in order to serve a number of social purposes, including the shaming of unscrupulous businesses and individuals and notices of escaped slaves (2009: 81–2). Wanted! posters, mugshots, and other examples of Lashmar's 'police photograph'—in the sense that police produced it—each, regardless of any more granular technical or administrative, are constitutive of and evidence of a distinct police power to criminalize via the visual.

Those same racialized and gendered origins of the Wanted! poster and the mugshot, which are themselves among the most iconic images and aesthetic modes flowing forth from police, are still plainly evident in the ongoing practice of photographing those targeted by or otherwise ensnared in police and the criminal justice system. As Linnemann and Wall (2013) describe, and as is discussed more comprehensively in Chapter 5, the visual forms taken on in public awareness efforts like the Faces of Meth campaign—which was designed from the outset as a way to use images of human suffering in order to further the aims and perspectives of police—continue to rely heavily on the logics of racialized photographic portraiture. These logics, of course, trace their own origins to posters advertising or warning of 'runaway slaves' (see generally Vimalassery 2016) and 'dangerous Indians' (see generally Francis 2012) posters that came to prominence so closely alongside police Wanted! posters that to try to disentangle them is impossible.

Finally, the enduring legacy of the mugshot, itself so seminal in the historical development of photography and so entangled with the visuality of police, emerges once again in the sorts of informal images often circulated by cops in the wake of police violence. Here we might consider the images of Trayvon Martin, the Black teen killed in Florida in February 2012 by George Zimmerman, a civilian who so strongly identified with the logics and power of police that he adopted the role, ultimately stalking and murdering the 17-year-old Martin. In the immediate wake of the murder, local and national media ran pictures of Martin and Zimmerman alongside coverage. The only image available of Zimmerman, though, was a police mugshot from an unrelated arrest for assault seven years prior to the murder of Martin, and so Zimmerman initially appeared to the public as an angry and scowling figure in an orange jumpsuit, a composition that ticks all of the boxes of precisely the category the image fits within: the classic mugshot. Zimmerman's defense team, recognizing that their client—a man of mixed heritage who nevertheless seemed to read to the public as white—was suddenly and, perhaps, unexpectedly on the receiving end of the power of the mugshot to construct the criminal, distributed alternative images of Martin to the media. The images, taken from

Martin's phone after the killing, showed a different side of Martin from that captured in images of the teen provided by his family. In these new images Martin appeared, basically, as what he was: a teenager in America playing with the costumes of adulthood and criminality, appearing to smoke marijuana and flash handguns. Quickly following the release of these images—accompanied, of course, by new images of Zimmerman in which the mugshot aesthetics of the first round of images, with all of their encoded racialization, are replaced by images of a somber, remorseful, and well-dressed man now fully racialized and encoded as 'white'—public perceptions seemed to swing in Zimmerman's favor, as was ultimately made clear in his acquittal.

Following the murder, and during Zimmerman's trial, the image played a central role not in establishing the facts of the case—the only surviving witness to the killing was Zimmerman, and no visual record existed—but in communicating to the public who the actors were. Those perceptions, though, certainly do not exist in a vacuum, somehow free from the long and powerful influence of the mugshot logics of race, gender, class, and grievability.

Body cameras, contemporary police images, and the police point of view

While we are surrounded, as described previously in this chapter, by images of police in the form of all manner of media and other visual artefacts of a culture of police, we are also surrounded with images from police. Of all of the various images from police that we encounter in our day-to-day lives, though, perhaps none has the contemporary salience or significance of the footage produced by police body cameras.

Although they had been piloted in the US and UK nearly a decade earlier, body-worn cameras—BWCs in the parlance of technocrats, police reformers, and academics alike—roared to the forefront of conversations about police violence in 2014, following the high-profile murder of Michael Brown, an unarmed Black American teenager, by Darren Wilson, a white cop, in Ferguson, Missouri (Schneider 2018: 450). A year after Brown's murder—a year that saw several other high-profile police killings—President Barack Obama pledged $75 million in federal funds for local police departments to equip police and police cars with an array of recording devices including dashcams and BWCs. While these measures were predictably popular among police reformers, who view the technology as an important step towards police accountability, they were equally popular, somewhat less predictably, among police themselves for their potential to be a 'safeguard against … scrutiny' (Wood 2016: 227). Here we find some evidence that police power is confident that footage of police violence captured on BWCs can always be framed and interpreted by police power itself as justifying police violence.

The hope, among reformers, of this particular technocratic refinement is obvious: that footage drawn from BWCs and police dashcams will aid in the identification and prosecution of police violence and misconduct. And, indeed, there is some reason to accept that logic. Since 2015, there has been nothing less than a deluge of images and video of police violence, too many to possibly watch, all captured from the precise point of view (POV) of police. While the corpus of these images grows exponentially, there remains little meaningful change to police and policing. This is explained, in part, by a foundational critique of police, which can be summarized as the insistence that police is not and never was intended to be contained or limited by law (Dubber 2005; McClanahan and Brisman 2016; Wall 2019),[7] and that in those rare moments when law does find itself capable of interceding in police power, it only does so after the fact.

We should also, though, consider the distinct aesthetic form and mode of images produced from the police POV. Here we can start by simply noting that the sheer volume of these images constitutes something like a canon. More importantly, though, we might begin to consider the ways in which that canon implies genre. Videos of the police POV, and in particular those videos and images that capture police killings of unarmed men, share huge amounts of connective tissue, all of them bound together in their own terrible genre. Flashing red and blue lights, wailing sirens, shouted commands, and pained and terrified calls for mercy are the hallmarks of the form.

That is the scene in the police video of the 2014 murder of 17-year-old Chicagoan Laquan McDonald, like so many others: a young man, perhaps troubled and certainly terrified, confronted by police. If you see the video, you know within the first few frames exactly how it will end, because you have seen it before, no different from any other cheap and thoughtless horror film. The murder, in which Jason Van Dyke emptied the 16-shot magazine of his police-issued pistol into Laquan McDonald, was captured from no less than six angles: five police videos, and at least one video from a nearby private security camera. When the police dashcam video was finally released, nearly one year after the killing, it plainly showed Laquan McDonald walking away from police when he was killed, and the criminal trial of Van Dyke—who had been charged with second-degree murder and a host of related charges, while three other cops involved in the shooting had been charged with offenses related to their failures to activate cameras and retain evidence— which was ongoing at the time, seemed as good as won for the prosecution. Van Dyke's defense, though, argued that the primary video, filmed by Van Dyke's dashcam, failed to show the scene from Van Dyke's perspective and, thus, failed to accurately capture the threat posed by Laquan McDonald. The jury ultimately found this argument uncompelling, though, and found Van Dyke guilty of the murder charge and 16 charges of battery, although they declined to convict on a charge of 'official misconduct', the only charge that was contingent on his role as a police officer. Illinois Attorney General Kwame Raoul mounted an effort to vacate the conviction and the attendant sentence—just over six years in prison—although his request was denied without comment by the Illinois Supreme Court.

The defense's argument in the case against Jason Van Dyke—that had Van Dyke been wearing a body camera, the footage would have proven that Laquan McDonald posed a meaningful threat, and that his murder was therefore justified—illustrates clearly the ways in which police BWCs are imagined only to report, capture, and reify the police POV. Here we should turn again to Mirzoeff's (2011a: 2–4) conceptualization of visuality as 'the authority to tell us to move on'— importantly, here Mirzoeff frames visuality explicitly as a police power—while reserving for itself that 'exclusive claim to be able to look'. The public interpretation of the event of Laquan McDonald's murder—despite being filtered through the ubiquitous head cops of the audience—is stripped of its own authoritative version of the killing, supplanted by, and because of, the historical and political and cultural authority of a police visuality that always produces and insists on its own point of view, its own interpretive processes. In their analysis of the police POV produced and reproduced in and by body camera images and footage, Carolyn McKay and Murray Lee (2020: 444) highlight the ways in which body camera aesthetics produce tensions between subject and object, and the ways in which the images produced by body cameras present an 'incomplete document' of the 'law enforcement event', which is almost always a murder.

There are also, though, other ways in which body cameras have failed to meaningfully arrest or intervene in police violence that have nothing to do with the images they produce. As we have seen time and again, police are routinely able to avoid video documentation by simply removing or turning off body cameras, or by concealing or destroying the footage they capture. Here, police exercise visuality in a different way, one in which the authority to see is buttressed by an architecture of total control over the production, dissemination, and very visibility of the image itself. Likewise, there are abundant 'new' police technologies, outside of the body-worn camera, that leverage the image into police service. One such technology, software firm Appriss' MobilePatrol, is noted by Kevin Revier (2020) as serving as a visual digital dashboard of sorts, compiling for police a range of data including images like mugshots and interactive 'crime hot-spot maps'. Appriss markets the app to police and the general public, promising that the technology can help police to 'rapidly and conveniently communicate vital public safety information'. As Revier describes, though, the app largely performs the same broad purpose as body cameras: to reify the police POV, and to 'assist in police-crafted image work' and 'advance symbolic policing' (2020: 315) in much the same ways as the police 'trophy shots' described previously.

Visual challenges to police power

While it might be consistently representative of it, the visual does not always support symbolic policing, police POV, and police image work and pacification. It is another tension of visuality that produces the other side of what we can perhaps most accurately imagine as the conflict between police and cameras (or, perhaps *more* accurately, police and the visual, given the ways in which police also reacts to non-photographic interpretations of or interventions into police practice), the side that emerges when police is suddenly confronted with the possibility of the production of a non-police visuality, a right to look asserted from below. Nowhere do we find more evidence of this conflict than in the moments in which police power is confronted by non-police cameras.

Just as we are all disquietingly familiar with the visual genre of police murder captured on the BWCs that reproduce the police POV, we also routinely encounter a distinctly policed POV in the recordings produced by the subjects of police power. This countervisuality, nearly as genre-constitutive as its police POV counterpart, is most plainly embodied in the efforts of activist groups like Copwatch and other organizations coalescing under the broad umbrella of the 'film the police' movement. These groups take as their raisons d'être the visual documentation of police activity, with members monitoring radio channels and city streets, seeking out police to film and photograph. Not surprisingly, this practice has been central in countless conflicts between police and their subjects, and one can quite easily pull up a seat, so to speak, and watch countless hours of online digital footage of explosions of police violence in response to camera-wielding activists.[8]

Police resistance to being filmed, described by Mary Bock (2016) as *sousveillance*, or a form of watching from below that seemingly inverts the traditional power relation of surveillance, is all but promised by the practice precisely because, as Bock notes, such forms of sousveillance have significant implications for theories of security, surveillance, and social control.

Resistance to being photographed, of course, is not limited to police confronted by camera-wielding activists. As Linda Mulcahy (2015) has described, there is a significant historical record of police captives wrenching away from the lens or otherwise resisting photographic capture, and obvious contemporary parallels exist in the various efforts made by activists and others to conceal their faces and other visual identifiers from police cameras. For a relation so shot through with drama, it is ironic—although wholly understandable—that both actors in that drama seem so prone to camera shyness.

Thinking about the police–image relation in the mode of visuality also encourages us to think again about the relation between the visual image and authority. Here we might again find an opportunity to tease out the elemental relation of cop and visual by noting that each, in its own way, both embodies and contains the entire conceptual field of authority. It makes sense then, given the history of the photographic image and its ties to police power, that the authoritative visuality of police and the broader visual authority of the image would exist in a cyclically and mutually reinforcing relation despite the ways in which cop watching complicates dominant notions of visual evidence (Bock 2016: 14).

Although there is undoubtedly a satisfying challenge to police power in the efforts of cop watchers, and while no critical criminologist worth their weight in salt would argue that police should be permitted to continue their work under full visual obscurity, the images produced by these efforts have evidently done quite little to constrain police violence. Just like the body-worn camera, the prevalence of the cop-watch camera has not resulted in the deconstruction of police's architecture of violence and killing, but instead in the construction of a new visuality of police that quickly finds the limits of its critical utility. As Wall and Linnemann (2014) note, in describing the so-called 'war on cameras' led by police against their watchers, the countersurveillance images produced by cop watchers are technologies of accountability. That accountability, though, is a 'decidedly liberal hope and one not nearly radical enough considering the structural force of police power' (Wall and Linnemann 2014: 136; see also Beutin 2017). Others, though, reject 'the complaint that photography's impact is more affect than action', such as Ariella Azoulay (2008), who argues for the 'continued relevance of the image for global accountability in the face of oppression' (Bock 2016: 17).

Part of the issue, it seems to me, is that hopes of accountability through video evidence of police violence always show a bad cop doing a bad thing while obscuring the structural and elemental violence of police. Because of the unmitigated success of the global police project of image work and the enduring strength of the police image, audiences of recorded police violence seem more or less content to see individual wrongdoing and deviance, and so even in video recordings of police killings police as a logic retains its legitimacy and heroism even while individual police find their image recast as villain. It is these enduring, sentimental images of police power, regardless of the site or context of their production, play an essential role in the ability of the state and police to absorb all criticism and crisis in the name of never-ending reform.

Counter police images and a countervisuality of police

The same visual fields in which police image work is undertaken, though, are also often marshalled against police power. As cultural criminologists have long argued, resistance to the classed, racialized, and gendered police order plays out largely on the registers of culture (see generally Ferrell 2007, 2019), and so the visual, with all of its cultural power and potency, clearly becomes an essential weapon in struggles against (police) power. In this sense, police is both affirmed and challenged by the image, a condition that is also, of course, largely shared by all other contemporary ideological formations.

Here we can consider the traditions of anti-police art, traditions that run across a broad spectrum of visual cultures both historic and contemporary. From Black Panther Party cultural minister and artist Emory Douglas' animalizing images of white police antagonists— which, at the direction of Black Panther founders Huey Newton and Bobby Seale, gave us the image of the cop as a pig, and of course the common epithet of 'pig' to refer derisively to police—to English street artist Banksy's playfully satirical takes on English bobbies in the 2000s in which the familiar 'friendly' copper stands next to crudely scrawled 'fuck the police' graffiti, to the graffiti, ubiquitous in the wake of street demonstrations, that rejects police power and cops, the visual registers of global culture are littered with images that can only be described as anti-police and anti-cop (see Figures 7.3 and 7.4).

Figure 7.3: Anti-police graffiti featuring pig imagery and 'fuck 12', a contemporary version of 'fuck the police'

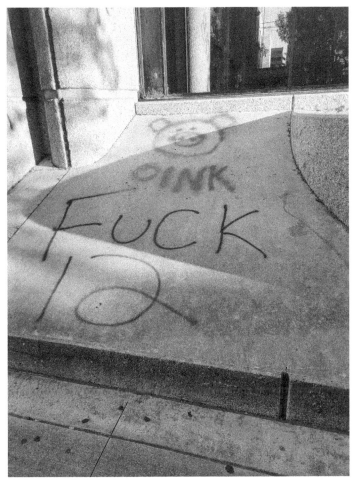

Note: Graffiti made on the Jefferson County District Court Hall of Justice in Louisville, Kentucky, during protests against police violence in the summer of 2020.

Source: Photo by the author.

As global uprisings against police began in the summer of 2020, it was immediately clear that the visual register would be a significant weapon in, and site of, the conflict between police power and its subjects. We might add, then, to our list of counter-police images, the ubiquitous anti-police graffiti that appeared, seemingly overnight, on the walls and streets of nearly every major American city. Bearing messages like 'fuck the police' or 'FTP', 'fuck 12' ('12' is contemporary slang for

Figure 7.4: Anti-police graffiti made during protests against police violence in Louisville, Kentucky, 2020

Source: Photo by the author.

police), and 'ACAB'—'all cops are bastards', an anti-police rallying cry most notably associated with the British punk rock movement but which actually significantly predates that distinct subcultural formation—much of this graffiti, like the images from Douglas, seems to recognize that leveraging vulgarity and profanity against the police demand of deference and politeness—what James C. Scott (1990) would call transgressing against the interactive 'public transcripts' that structure unequal relations—strikes at the heart of police power. Plenty of criminologists have taken an interest in the visual by way of graffiti (as described in earlier chapters), and that interest might be further focused on explicitly anti-police graffiti in order to further theorize police power through the (often visual, and occasionally countervisual) cultural artefacts of a culture of police.

Like the prison described in the previous chapter, to negate the vision and image of police, even if only in the imagination, is difficult. The eyes we see from are, after all, shared by the cops in our heads, and so to see the world without police in it, or to see the world through eyes not captured by police logics, is not as simple as turning away from the material manifestations of images of police (which, of course, would be wholly impossible itself, given the ubiquity of those images).

Finally, police power has also had the logics of the Wanted! poster turned against itself as activists and street artists produce counter-Wanted! posters featuring the names and faces of cops. As Stuart Schrader describes (2020), these sorts of 'unofficial wanted posters ... provide a window onto subterranean social struggles' while demonstrating the ways in which counter-imaging and countervisual techniques can be instrumental in 'turning hieroglyphs of state power'—mugshots—'against state power' itself. This mode of the counter-image was deployed recently in Louisville, Kentucky, for example, in posters that appeared in the city (and in digital versions of the same image that have circulated online in social media) calling for the arrest and prosecution of the police involved in the murder of Breonna Taylor, the young Black woman killed in her home by police in March of 2020 (see Figure 7.5).

While we might celebrate the critical aesthetics of the sorts of anti-police imagery described and illustrated here—and, to be clear, there is plenty of potency and value in these sorts of images that lay bare the ridiculousness or violence of police, or simply responds to the police demand for respect and genuflection with vulgarity and insult—we should also note that, as with the sorts of counter-carceral images described previously, there is a distinction between the counter-image and a countervisuality. In pursuit of a more fully formed countervisuality of police, then, those material counter-images of police must give way to a visionary process of imagining—and bringing into being—not just a world without police, but a world beyond police.

Conclusion

As this chapter has illustrated, there is some analytical potential in thinking about the intersection(s) of police and the visual in order to more fully and critically theorize police power. Some progress has already been made in that direction, too, of course, and some of that progress has come from within criminology. It is, all the same, my contention that if any criminology—visual or otherwise—is to make a worthwhile contribution to the theorization of police, it must first make some fundamental recognitions. Chief among these is that the elemental role and purpose of police always has been and remains the production, maintenance, and reproduction of a social order favorable to capital, property, and patriarchal social relations. Those essential processes in the police's production of order are all undertaken, in part, on the cultural registers of a visual economy through measures like

Figure 7.5: Counter-image produced in the wake of the police killing of Breonna Taylor in Louisville, Kentucky, 2020

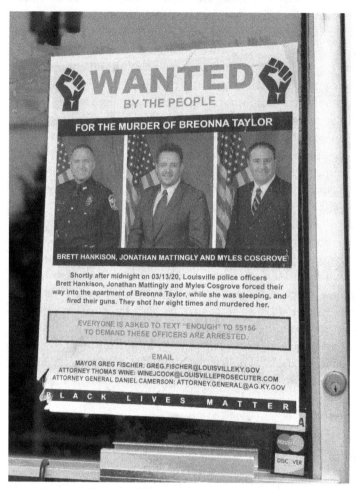

Source: Courtesy of Josh McClellan.

police image work, wherein the figure of police always lurks in the shadows, and so perhaps we might also insist that any critical theoretical analysis of police consider the spectacular power of the visual and its role in the spectacular power of police.

Visual criminology is, it would seem, well positioned to reckon and grapple with the various moments in which police and the image intersect. Potentially fertile avenues for criminological research may be identified or realized, including in research that examines the role of police images in police legitimacy; the role of digital archives in constructing and policing a criminal class; the ways in which visual surveillance technologies condition policing; the role of the image in the processes of criminal racialization; or the construction of a countervisuality of police, to name but a few. It is also likely that, as the routine visualization of police continues—in the sense that new visual techniques and technologies are constantly acting on police power and practice—new intersections of police and image will emerge, and they, too, will necessitate new visual approaches to criminological research.

There is also, as described in this chapter, a great temptation to assume that the various sorts of visual challenges to police power—the critical and teasing images, the digital proliferation of hours and hours of recorded police violence and killing, the rise of activist efforts to turn the lens on police power, or technocratic police reforms like body-worn cameras—will meaningfully curb or slow police violence. Leaving aside, in the interest of space and focus, the elemental and ever-present violence of police, I simply note that the rise of each of these techniques and technologies has been accompanied only by an intensification of the very modes of police violence these images seek to arrest. These visually focused efforts at addressing the problem of police rely far too much on liberal procedural justice and systemic checks on power to address fundamentally violent ideological institutions like police.

Police power, with all of its built-in dramatics and necessary image-work, lives and dies by the image. Police images—mugshots, Wanted! posters, thin blue line products, the entire canon of police in cinema and literature and art, and footage of police killings captured by police body-worn cameras, for example—are marshalled within a visual culture of police to produce, reproduce, or reify police power and logics. While some images—ACAB and FTP and 'fuck 12' graffiti, footage from Copwatch and other efforts to document police violence, and, at times, the same footage of police killings captured by body-worn cameras that also affirms police power—might present a countervisual challenge that appears to destabilize visual police power, these efforts rarely if ever overcome the intense power of the police image.

The inability of the image to intervene in police, though, does not indicate the inability of police to intervene in the image. Rather, as described throughout this chapter, police inserts itself—its POV and its visuality—into every image and every scene, every photograph and painting and film. Whether we encounter images of police or police images, or even countervisual images critical of police, that essential relation remains the same. It is perhaps adequate, then, for a visual criminology of police to conclude by simply noting that police power constitutes, produces, infects, and—of course—polices all visual regimes.

8

New Horizons in Visual Criminology

This book began with the killing of George Floyd by cops in Minneapolis, Minnesota in the spring of 2020. It is fitting, then, that it ends more or less there, too. Instead, however, of the immediate particular circumstances of George Floyd's murder—the knee in his back, the violent disinterest of Derek Chauvin and his coworker accomplices on the scene, or the pleas of bystanders, with their mobile phone cameras rolling, to the police to stop, to allow George Floyd to breathe—I end on what came next, as the world was confronted yet again with the painfully familiar image of the police violence of racial capitalism: a Black man killed by the state.

As this book has argued, described, and demonstrated, over the previous seven chapters, there is ample opportunity to find some criminological and sociological truth in the image, and in the ways in which we produce and employ and understand it. Images constitute and condition the social worlds of crime, harm, and justice, and we live our lives more or less immersed in their spectacle. But when George Floyd died the world did not just 'see it happen': George Floyd's killing, like those before it, is not simply seen in the footage of his murder, it is *felt*. It is not only images of a police murder that are produced when the cameras roll, it is the sounds of a murder. It is George Floyd's dying plea for his mother, or 26-year-old Daniel Shaver begging in a hotel corridor for clear instruction seconds before being hit five times with shots from Mesa, Arizona cop Phillip Brailsford's AR-15 rifle, on which Brailsford had carefully inscribed 'you're fucked' in an ornate script. Seeing George Floyd with his face on the pavement, or Daniel Shaver pressed against the drab hotel carpet, we *feel* some fraction of their distress and the tactile experience of their last moments. Watching these videos a second, third, fourth time, some of us taste bile and rage rising in our throats. In the wake of their deaths, people go to the streets, where they smell and taste and feel tear gas and pepper spray and hear sirens and bullhorns, gunshots and explosions.

It is, then, far more than the visual that constructs or constitutes our experiences and knowledge of crime and justice. This short final chapter takes that as its starting point, and details and describes the limitations of visual criminology while at once reaffirming its necessity, utility, and potential. I begin with a brief description of some limitations of visual criminology relating to issues of ocularcentrism and sensorial hierarchies. Following that, I describe the ways that visual criminology might continue to develop alongside ongoing cultural criminological interest in the spatial forces of crime and culture, and the ways in which visual criminology continues to have significant potential as a distinctly public and accessible criminological variant. The book concludes with some final thoughts on the relation between the visual and our affective condition, describing some ways in which our criminological horizons might be expanded by increased attention to the ways in which how we feel about crime, harm, and justice are conditioned by the image and the visual.

The most pressing and restrictive limitation of visual criminology is also the most obvious: it is visual. By this I mean to indicate that visual criminology suffers from the same problems of ocularcentrism—privileging sight above the other senses, and orienting knowledge around vision—that have haunted the production of knowledge since at least the early days of Greek philosophy, where observability in an almost strictly visual sense became an immovable feature of empiricism. Plato, after all, made the unequivocal claim, in fourth-century BCE Athens, that among the senses 'the sight ... is the source of the greatest benefit to us' (see generally Alexander 1918: 10). For Plato and other early philosophers and systems of knowledge, sight was exceptional in part because it revealed important conceptual fields like order and nature and thus produced a certain power to 'regulate our own vagaries'. Others, like Heraclitus, who wrote some four centuries before Plato that 'those things of which there is sight, hearing, knowledge' were what he 'honored most', although he also includes hearing in his formulation, even Heraclitus would quickly correct himself and affirm the superiority of vision, noting that 'the eyes are more exact witnesses than the ears' (Graham 2007).

From these moments in early Greek philosophy onward, there has been a peculiar—albeit understandable and, it seems, inescapable—tendency to value the visual over the other senses. Khazam (2014) deconstructs the 'hierarchy of the senses' that has stood since Ancient Greece, with Western society ranking sight, hearing, touch, taste, and smell 'according to their "perceived epistemological importance"' (Buccafusco 2006: 1140). Although this hierarchy has been historically and socially constructed, with the bases for the favored and the unfavored having no real essential foundation, 'sight' has routinely been privileged as 'the noblest of senses', a tendency influencing criminology today as much as it influenced Plato, Socrates and Heraclitus. That tendency, though, has not been without critique. Jay (1988, 1991) has decried the ocularcentrism that characterized scopic regimes in the wake of Cartesian thought, while Rukavina (2013) describes the ways in which ocularcentrism is reflective not only of the privileging of one sense, but of a broader and more problematic privileging of Western thought.

Another problem–opportunity for visual criminology is presented by new and emergent technologies that act on the image. While much has been made, in media and the academy alike, about the rise of a so-called 'post-truth' era, the bulk of these concerns surround narrative media. That distinction, though, is likely soon to evaporate—perhaps even before this book is printed, given the rapidity of technological advancement—with the inevitable rise of 'deep-fake' technologies, which will very soon cast the specter of doubt over *all* images. Perhaps, then, we shall see a reordering of Debord's useful maxim, one in which the false becomes an element of the true rather than vice versa. Visual criminology, in light of these developments, might find itself tasked with grappling with the implications of a technological shift that renders the evidentiary power of the image moot, or at least calls it into serious question.

Among the most essential tasks for visual criminology, clearly, is to be mindful of the ways in which ocularcentrism and the privileging of sight over the other senses and non-sensory knowledge might reproduce or empower the harmful dimensions of a hierarchy of sensorial knowledge. Visual criminology (and other critical criminologies), much to its credit, has for as long as it has been on the scene made note of the significance of non-visual and extra-visual sensory modalities (see generally Brown and Carrabine 2019), including touch, smell, taste, and sound (see generally McClanahan and South 2020). This tendency is even more pronounced in cultural criminology, where there is a longstanding interest in the sensual dimensions of crime and criminality (see generally Katz 1988; Ferrell 2004; King and Maruna 2020). Recently, some visual criminologists and others have sounded calls for an explicitly sensory criminology, one concerned with other sensorial modalities in the same general ways in which visual criminology concerns itself with the visual. Examples of research in this area are not at all few and far between, with sound and acoustic space emerging as central and essential sites of interest (see generally, for example, Russell 2020; Russell and Mae 2020).

As described in the opening chapters, visual criminology grew, in large part, from the eclectic gardens of cultural criminology, and it was from cultural criminology that visual criminology adopted its foundational interest in the intersection(s) of crime and cultural products and production. Cultural criminology also, though, provides a tether that continues to bind visual criminology to some distinctly criminological ways of thinking about space. These geographic tendencies have played a significant role in the construction of the visual criminology we find before us today (as well, for that matter, as the other non-visual sensory criminologies described earlier, which also have space and place among their chief conceptual concerns). While traditional criminology typically employs the categories and concepts of space and place as part of, to use an obvious example, crime mapping and other basic means of combining criminological and spatial knowledges, cultural criminology draws significantly on cultural and human geography in order to consider the ways in which space and place act on crime and culture as co-constitutive forces (see generally Hayward 2012).

While 'space' is commonly employed as a conceptual category in cultural criminology in immaterial ways—cultural criminologists often train their attention on categories like cultural space (Ferrell 1999: 396) that may have geographic dimensions and iterations, but are not strictly material—it has also been used in more material ways. This distinction is not entirely important, though, as both conceptual and material ideas about space and place are implicated the processes of vision: we imagine and experience space and place through the complex and interwoven processes of the senses, and sight and vision play as important a role as ever. Examples of the geographic tendency in criminology include work that describes the ways in which protest and resistance function in and across urban space (Naegler 2012), the ways in which crime is governed through spatial exclusion (Hayward 2004), the social practice of exploring 'forbidden, forgotten or otherwise off-limits places' (Kindynis 2017), cartography and its relations to criminology (Kindynis 2014: 222), and the ways in which authority is spatially constituted (Ferrell 1997a: 29).

A consistent strength throughout cultural criminology concerns its holistic disciplinary attention to the dynamics of public space, particularly urban space.[1] Much of the cultural criminology cited and engaged with here, for example, takes 'the city' as one of its chief sites of inquiry, often as part of a larger criminological analysis of cultural practices like graffiti writing that condition and configure our understandings of crime as a force with spatial implications. Moving forward, it seems likely that graffiti and street art and other spatialized cultural practices will continue to provide fruitful intersections of visual and cultural criminologies.

This book has also demonstrated that criminological images are produced not by or for criminologists, and that the processes of visualization that constitute visual criminology are not limited to criminology and criminologists. Instead, the spectacle is made up almost entirely, in our dizzyingly fast-paced mediated and globalized world, of images of crime and justice and harm, and so our entire visual atmosphere is, more or less, conditioned by them. Any criminologist reading this knows well the allure of special knowledge about crime and harm, but the truth of it is that we social scientists are no more equipped to rend justice or knowledge from the image than anyone else. The criminological knowledge that has everyday value—knowledge that compels us to move through space in certain ways, to lock our doors and expect the worst, to pursue justice, to speak or not speak, to look or not look—is not built only in the halls of universities: it is formulated in the sensory processes of the visual, and it is expressed and communicated in the spectacle of popular culture. For Nicky Rafter (2007: 403), whose vision has been so central in visual criminology's development and in this book, there was an intense tie binding visual criminology and popular criminology, which, she argued, brought 'to bear ethical, philosophical and psychological perspectives beyond the scope of academic research', and which, in her view, could 'invigorate … criminology itself'. For Rafter, the cinema was the most significant source of popular criminological knowledge. The visual criminology that has developed in the intervening decade and a half, though, has built on that foundation, and we now find ourselves with a robust, vibrant, and critical way of seeing that imbues with rich criminological meaning the images that surround us and the visual processes that make and take them in.

Finally, it is worth noting, as several others have, that the deluge of images we endure is always growing in quantity and intensity alike; our devices and our ever-increasing technical ability to take in images ensure endless visual content, and the ever-changing modes of aesthetics ensure a degree of vertigo. In part, this raises new questions about the velocity of contemporary images, and the ways in which the increasingly digitized landscape of the visual allows for new visual flows and interactions, new encounters with the image. An illustrative example, and one that will return us one last time to the killings of George Floyd and others that have produced some of the essential contemporary criminological images taken up in this book, is the image in Figure 8.1, taken during a Black Lives Matter demonstration in Berlin, Germany in the summer of 2020.

Figure 8.1: Sign for Breonna Taylor at a Black Lives Matter protest in Berlin, Germany, 2020

Source: Courtesy of Sybille Reuter/Alamy Stock Photo.

The sign reads, alongside a soft pastel drawing of a smiling Breonna Taylor:

> *From Berlin to Louisville*
> *Justice for Breonna*
> *Say her name.*

Conclusion

As I write this in September 2020, some 80 miles away from my office, the city of Louisville, Kentucky, where Breonna Taylor was killed by police in early 2020, braces for the unrest that will inevitably follow the Kentucky Attorney General's announcement, made just moments ago, that none of the cops involved in her death will be charged. People around the world will see and hear the announcement, and will go to the streets in protest. There, they will be met with the menacing thousand-yard stare of police and the visuality of state power, built in part by decades of a global drug war that has been fought on the visual register. They will confront the toxic and suffocating conditions of a material environment ravaged by climate change and the other vast ecological harms wrought by global capitalism. They will, some of them, awaken later in jail cells, and later still in prison cells, and later still under the administrative and panoptic gaze of e-carceration monitors and other contemporary modes of control, exclusion, and punishment. Their experiences of harm and justice and crime, like all of ours, will be mediated in and by the visual. Of course, millions more will watch, the velocity of the contemporary criminological image sending it rocketing around the world and on to our screens and into our imaginations.

This will be repeated, around the world, either in Breonna's name or in the name of another victim of state violence, or in the names of all of us, really, who are made to endure the spectacular violence that we see, always, before us. Another face and another name will circulate around the planet, and we will suddenly all know a new layer, a new tragedy. All of this will happen by the image. It will be photographed and those photographs will become evidence and knowing. It will be visualized, and through those processes it will become material. It will, also, of course, be contested in the image and the visual, and new tensions will emerge even as old ones disappear under the unbearable weight of historically accumulated images of crime, harm, and justice. By the image, Breonna Taylor will be in Berlin, Eyad al-Hallaq will be in Louisville, and George Floyd will be in Bethlehem, and in each they will all be joined by masses of the living, spectators moved by the images and imaginaries of their lives and deaths.

For now, then, it seems we will continue to meet spectacle with gaze, to know and understand our social, cultural, and material worlds through the processes of the visual, and to be surrounded, set upon on all sides by the criminological image. Crime and harm and justice and so much more will continue to be constituted and contested in the senses and on the field of the image, and so it is the task of a visual criminology to take them seriously, and to find in them insight and knowledge, some more complete understanding of our condition.

Notes

Chapter 1

1   The Situationists—and particularly Debord's (2012) seminal *Society of the Spectacle*—take a prominent role in much cultural criminology, but perhaps most particularly in Ferrell's influential article 'Boredom, crime and criminology' (2004), in which Ferrell makes a compelling case that a Situationist-inspired cultural criminology constitutes an active resistance to the 'institutionalized boredom' of mainstream criminology. For a thorough elaboration on the ways in which critical criminology has been informed by the Frankfurt School and by critical theory more broadly, see Majid Yar's 'Critical criminology, critical theory and social harm' (2012).

2   The implications of each for a visual criminology are discussed more thoroughly in the final chapter of this book.

3   Lombroso's work, of course, would also be instrumental in developing the rotten pseudoscience of race and in constructing racialized difference in the political imagination of the Western world, and it continues to condition, sometimes reflexively, huge swathes of public and formal criminological thinking. Quoting Gilroy, Kate West has described the centrality of Lombroso's work to 'the project to make the idea of "race" epistemologically correct' (Gilroy 2000: 58, quoted in West 2017: 273). Lombroso's visual work, then, is not simply a flight of fancy from the 'father of criminology', but rather a central part of a research agenda and method that continues to condition the intersection(s) of race, crime, harm, justice, and the image.

Chapter 2

1   'Ways of seeing' here, as almost anywhere the phrase is found, recalls the deeply influential work of John Berger, the artist, author, critic, and poet, who in 1972 produced, alongside Mike Dibb, a series of four 30-minute television episodes exploring the relationship between visual images and aesthetics and ideology, with a particular emphasis on the ways in which ideological formations were made and communicated through image work and the work of the image (Berger 2008). In that same year, Berger and his colleagues supplemented it with a book by the same name that would go on to be a huge influence in visual studies and art criticism, as well as a foundational text for some feminist theorists interested in the role of mediated images in patriarchal and unequal social relations (Berger 2003, 2018; see also Jones 2003a, 2003b).

2   A thorough accounting of the visual turn in the social sciences and humanities is, unfortunately but obviously, entirely outside of the scope of this book. Such an account, though, would certainly be useful and interesting to anyone exploring visual criminology, and so I would guide readers to Jay (2002a, 2002b) and Pauwels (2000).

3   It is worth mentioning here that much of the analytical and visual work of *Righteous Dopefiend* is in the ways in which the text and images relate to one another. As previously mentioned, there is always a risk in a visual social science that the visual will be reduced to the image—the window-dressing effect—and *Righteous Dopefiend*

stands as an example of an approach to photo ethnography that mostly successfully resists the urge to think *around* images instead of thinking *about* the visual.

4   Here we can also understand Carrabine's 'spectacles of suffering' as in conversation with Foucault's (1977: 33) 'spectacle of the scaffold' through which Foucault metaphorized the execution as a 'political spectacle of intense pain that reaffirms the body of the king and hence the body politic' (Hutson 2005: 33).

5   For a fantastic and thorough exploration of the relationship between the visual and the evidentiary, see Dufour and Delage (2015).

Chapter 3

1   Here, we should be careful to keep in mind that the very idea of a single canon of art is deeply problematic in myriad ways, chief among them because of the canon's ability and tendency to include only Western art, or art that reflects Western ideological tendencies and normative structures while excluding any art that might challenge or otherwise contradict those same tendencies and structures.

Chapter 4

1   'None' is likely not strictly correct here. As Lam and Tegelberg (2020: 111) describe, the image of the polar bear has, in fact, been racialized, by way of 'an association between the bears, light and whiteness, where the bear's white fur is reflected by and reflective of the whiteness of the Arctic snowscape' in a way that suggests the reinforcement of dominant visual cultural narratives of race that bind white, whiteness, purity, and cleanliness in the public visual imagination (see generally Razack 2002, 2004; Zimring 2017).

Chapter 6

1   Two quite obvious exceptions to this are the fields of green criminology and situational crime prevention. In the case of the former, though, space and place are generally only necessarily addressed as one dimension among many of human–environment interactions and as important sites of harm (see, for example, Brisman et al 2014; Hayward 2016a, 2016b). In the case of the latter, space and place are rigid and fixed categories that bear little resemblance to their counterparts in human and cultural geography. Despite several calls for a more spatially attuned criminology (see generally Ferrell 1999; Hayward 2012, 2016a, 2016b; Brisman et al 2014; McClanahan 2019; McClanahan and South 2020; Scott and Staines 2020), criminology continues to inadequately theorize or even consider space and place.

2   It is worth noting that, without any sort of systematic analysis, the image and aesthetics of the Scandinavian model of penal design and construction fails to satisfy the punitive spirit of American spectators, who more often than not seem to conflate the 'humanistic' design language of Scandinavian carcerality to a less effective, less-just form of punishment; for some punitive appetites, years locked in a cell that is not aggressively designed to maximize pain and discomfort wherever possible is hardly punishment at all, with commentators frequently suggesting that prisoners in places like Iceland and Norway live in better conditions than many of the working and working poor of the rest of the world.

3   We might also note here that Story's aim of recasting the prison and carceral impulse as 'strange' seems to share some common concerns with Fiddler's analysis of the prison as a cinematic device through the lens of Freud's 'uncanny', and that, first, the tendency to understand the prison through the language of the 'weird' 'uncanny' and 'eerie'—all overlapping concepts—is a real one (expressed also in Vidler 1992; Jewkes and Linnemann 2017; Puddu and Meloni 2017; Fredriksson 2019; McClanahan 2021; and surely more); and second, there seems to be a growing criminological interest in these concepts that is emerging both from and alongside existing streams of visual criminology (see Fiddler et al 2021).

Chapter 7

1   The Comaroffs also gesture towards the visual dimensions of both visibility and invisibility that condition policing by noting respectively, among other things, '*images* of crime and policing' (2004: 802, emphasis added) and '*specters* of illegality' (2004: 801, emphasis mine). Similarly, others have noted and described the dramas of police and policing using Erving Goffman's (1959) metaphor of backstage and frontstage lives (see generally Holdaway (1980), who describes the ways that the stage metaphor governs the material space of the police station, and Millie (2012), who questions the role of the front stage–back stage distinction in the architecture of the police station and its role in reassuring the public of their safety.

2   These categories, of course, are not fixed and not comprehensive: most or many images, as we shall see, fit comfortably within either, and one could certainly further construct and refine much more comprehensive categories. For the purposes of this chapter, though, it seems a sufficient distinction.

3   Among the central powers of police, as described by Chamayou (2012) and Wall (2013), is the power to hunt. While it is far outside the scope of this chapter or book to develop it here, it is worth noting that hunting is also, of course, a technique and technology that underscores the visual and sensory power of police (McClanahan and South 2020).

4   It is fitting, given the dramatics of police and policing, that the 'cop in the head' has been considered most seriously by drama theorists (see generally Boal and Epstein 1990).

5   Bertillon, who was working in roughly the time of Lombroso, was like his Italian contemporary heavily involved and invested in the development of an early visual criminological enterprise, and the work of both men is deeply implicated in the development of so-called 'race science'. Bertillon's work would also give rise to the formal practice of fingerprinting, as well as broader archival and cataloging practices producing the kinds of formal and state records that Frantz Fanon called the *mise en fiches de l'homme*—a record of man—and which he claimed were a constitutive characteristic of modernity (Browne 2015: 5).

6   As noted elsewhere in this text, some criminologists (Rafter 2005; Rafter and Ystehede 2010; West 2017, 2019) have described Lombroso—despite his contemporary position as a criminological pariah—as a pioneering visual criminologist.

7   This point, perhaps obviously, has clear implications for police reform, in that it largely insists that police reform is more or less impossible, as it relies entirely on a power from which police is always expressly shielded.

[8] Wall and Linnemann (2014: 134–5) offer a useful list and analysis of several of these moments of confrontation.

Chapter 8

[1] This tendency in cultural criminology has led some to question the field's preoccupation with 'the urban' and work towards a broader cultural criminology of space that makes more effort to account for non-urban spaces (Brisman et al 2014).

References

Abbott, R. (2020). Artificial intelligence, big data and intellectual property: Protecting computer generated works in the United Kingdom. In T. Aplin (ed) *Research Handbook on Intellectual Property and Digital Technologies*. Cheltenham: Edward Elgar Publishing, pp. 322–37.

Alexander, H.B. (1918). Plato's conception of the cosmos. *The Monist*, 28(1), 1–24.

Almond, B. Bailey, D. and Neumeyer, K. (2017). *Moral Uncertainty: Inside the Rodney King Juries*. Andalou Books.

Alvelos, H. (2004). The desert of imagination in the city of signs: Cultural implications of sponsored transgression and branded graffiti. In J. Ferrell, K. Hayward, W. Morrison, and M. Presdee (eds) *Cultural Criminology Unleashed*. London: The Glass House Press, pp. 181–91.

Armstrong, J. (2010). On the possibility of spectral ethnography. *Cultural Studies? Critical Methodologies*, 10(3), 243–50.

Azoulay, A. (2008). *The Civil Contract*. New York, NY: Zone Books.

Azoulay, A. (2015). *Civil Imagination: A Political Ontology of Photography*. London: Verso Books.

Banks, M. and Morphy, H. (eds) (1999). *Rethinking Visual Anthropology*. New Haven, CT: Yale University Press.

Bartel, R.L. (2005). When the heavenly gaze criminalises: Satellite surveillance, land clearance regulation and the human-nature relationship. *Current Issues in Criminal Justice*, 16(3), 322–39.

Barthes, R. (1972). *Mythologies* (trans. A. Lavers). New York, NY: Hill & Wang.

Becker, H. (1979). Do photographs tell the truth? In T.D. Cook and C.S. Reichardt (eds) *Qualitative and Quantitative Methods in Evaluation Research*. Thousand Oaks, CA: Sage Publications.

Becker, H.S. (1995). Visual sociology, documentary photography, and photojournalism: It's (almost) all a matter of context. *Visual Studies*, 10(1–2), 5–14.

Becker, H.S. (2002). Visual evidence: A seventh man, the specified generalization, and the work of the reader. *Visual Studies*, 17(1), 3–11.

Beirne, P. (2013). Hogarth's animals. *Journal of Animal Ethics*, 3(2), 133–62.

Beirne, P. (2014). *Hogarth's Art of Animal Cruelty: Satire, Suffering and Pictorial Propaganda*. New York, NY: Springer.

Beirne, P. (2015). Seeing Hogarth's animal images. In P. Beirne, *Hogarth's Art of Animal Cruelty: Satire, Suffering and Pictorial Propaganda*. London: Palgrave Pivot, pp. 10–43.

Beirne, P. (2018). Hogarth's patriotic animals: Bulldogs, beef, Britannia! In *Murdering Animals*. London: Palgrave Macmillan, pp. 135–64.

Beller, J. (2012). *The Cinematic Mode of Production: Attention Economy and the Society of the Spectacle*. Lebanon, NH: UPNE.

Bendell, J. (2018). *Deep Adaptation: A Map for Navigating Climate Tragedy*. IFLAS Occasional Paper 2. Ambleside: IFLAS, University of Cumbria.

Benjamin, W. (2008). *The Work of Art in the Age of Mechanical Reproduction*. London: Penguin.

Berger, J. (2003). From ways of seeing. In A. Jones (ed) *The Feminism and Visual Culture Reader*. East Sussex: Psychology Press, pp. 37–40.

Berger, J. (2008). *Ways of Seeing*. London: Penguin.

Berger, J. (2016). *Portraits*. London: Verso Books.

Berger, J. (2018). *Landscapes: John Berger on Art*. London: Verso Books.

Bernstein, L. (2010). *America is the Prison: Arts and Politics in Prison in the 1970s*. Chapel Hill, NC: University of North Carolina Press.

Beutin, L.P. (2017). Racialization as a way of seeing: The limits of counter-surveillance and police reform. *Surveillance & Society*, 15(1), 5–20.

Biber, K. (2007). *Captive images: Race, Crime, Photography*. Abingdon: Routledge.

Biber, K. (2013). In crime's archive: The cultural afterlife of criminal evidence. *The British Journal of Criminology*, 53(6), 1033–49.

Biber, K. (2015). Peeping: Open justice and law's voyeurs. In C. Sharp and M. Leiboff (eds) *Cultural Legal Studies*. Abingdon: Routledge, pp. 178–200.

Biber, K. (2018). *In Crime's Archive: The Cultural Afterlife of Evidence*. London: Taylor & Francis.

Biber, K. and Dalton, D. (2009). Making art from evidence: Secret sex and police surveillance in the tearoom. *Crime, Media, Culture*, 5(3), 243–67.

Biber, K. and Luker, T. (2014). Evidence and the archive: Ethics, aesthetics, and emotion. *Australian Feminist Law Journal*, 40, 1.

Boal, A. and Epstein, S. (1990). The cop in the head: Three hypotheses. *TDR (1988–)*, 34(3), 35–42.

Bock, M.A. (2016). Film the police! Cop-watching and its embodied narratives. *Journal of Communication*, 66(1), 13–34.

Bond, H. (2012). *Lacan at the Scene*. Cambridge, MA: MIT Press.

Bonds, A. (2006). Profit from punishment? The politics of prisons, poverty and neoliberal restructuring in the rural American Northwest. *Antipode*, 38(1), 174–7.

Bonds, A. (2009). Discipline and devolution: Constructions of poverty, race, and criminality in the politics of rural prison development. *Antipode*, 41(3), 416–38.

Bourdieu, P. (1990). *The Logic of Practice*. Stanford, CA: Stanford University Press.

Bourgois, P.I. and Schonberg, J. (2009). *Righteous Dopefiend* (Vol. 21). Berkeley, CA: University of California Press.

Boxall, K. and Ralph, S. (2009). Research ethics and the use of visual images in research with people with intellectual disability. *Journal of Intellectual and Developmental Disability*, 34(1), 45–54.

Brisman, A. (2014). The visual acuity of climate change. In P. Davies, P. Francis and T. Wyatt (eds) *Invisible Crimes and Social Harms*. Basingstoke: Palgrave Macmillan, pp. 61–80.

Brisman, A. (2015). 'Multicolored' green criminology and climate change's achromatopsia. *Contemporary Justice Review*, 18(2), 178–96.

Brisman, A. (2017a). On narrative and green cultural criminology. *International Journal for Crime, Justice and Social Democracy*, 6(2), 64.

Brisman, A. (2017b). Representations of environmental crime and harm: A green cultural criminological perspective on *Human-Altered Landscapes*. In M. Brown and E. Carrabine (eds) *Routledge International Handbook of Visual Criminology*. Abingdon: Routledge, pp. 523–39.

Brisman, A. and South, N. (2013). A green-cultural criminology: An exploratory outline. *Crime, Media, Culture*, 9(2), 115–35.

Brisman, A. and South, N. (2014). *Green cultural criminology: Constructions of environmental harm, consumerism, and resistance to ecocide*. Abingdon: Routledge.

Brisman, A and South, N. (2016). Green cultural criminology, intergenerational (in)equity and 'life stage dissolution'. In M. Hall, T. Wyatt, N. South, A. Nurse, G. Potter, and J. Maher (eds) *Greening Criminology in the 21st Century: Contemporary Debates and Future Directions in the Study of Environmental Harm*. Abingdon: Routledge, pp. 219–31.

Brisman, A., McClanahan, B. and South, N. (2014). Toward a green-cultural criminology of 'the rural'. *Critical Criminology*, 22(4), 479–94.

Brisman, A., McClanahan, B., South, N. and Walters, R. (2018). *Water, Crime and Security in the Twenty-First Century: Too Dirty, Too Little, Too Much*. New York, NY: Springer.

Brown, M. (2009). *The Culture of Punishment: Prison, Society, and Spectacle*. New York, NY: New York University Press.

Brown, M. (2013). Penal spectatorship and the culture of punishment. In D. Scott (ed) *Why Prison?* Cambridge: Cambridge University Press, pp. 108–24.

Brown, M. (2014). Visual criminology and carceral studies: Counter-images in the carceral age. *Theoretical Criminology*, 18(2), 176–97.

Brown, M. (2017). Penal optics and the struggle for the right to look: Visuality and prison tourism in the carceral era. In J. Wilson, S. Hodgkinson, J. Piché, and K. Walby (eds) *The Palgrave Handbook of Prison Tourism*. London: Palgrave Macmillan, pp. 153–67.

Brown, M. (2020). The challenge of informative justice: Insurgent knowledge and public criminology. In K. Henne and R. Shah (eds) *Routledge Handbook of Public Criminologies*. Abingdon: Routledge, pp. 49–190.

Brown, M. and Carrabine, E. (2017). Introducing visual criminology. In M. Brown and E. Carrabine (eds) *Routledge International Handbook of Visual Criminology*. Abingdon: Routledge, pp. 1–9.

Brown, M. and Carrabine, E. (2019). The critical foundations of visual criminology: The state, crisis, and the sensory. *Critical Criminology*, 27(1), 191–205.

Brown, M. and Rafter, N. (2013). Genocide films, public criminology, collective memory. *The British Journal of Criminology*, 53(6), 1017–32.

Browne, S. (2015). *Dark Matters: On the Surveillance of Blackness*. Durham, NC: Duke University Press.

Buccafusco, C.J. (2006). On the legal consequences of sauces: Should Thomas Keller's recipes be per se copyrightable? *Cardozo Arts & Entertainment Law Journal*, 24, 1122–56.

Budig, K., Diez, J., Conde, P., Sastre, M., Hernán, M. and Franco, M. (2018). Photovoice and empowerment: Evaluating the transformative potential of a participatory action research project. *BMC Public Health*, 18(1), 1–9.

Butler, J. (2006). *Precarious Life: The Powers of Mourning and Violence*. London: Verso Books.

Butler, J. (2016). *Frames of War: When is Life Grievable?* London: Verso Books.

Campbell, D. (2007). Geopolitics and visuality: Sighting the Darfur conflict. *Political Geography*, 26(4), 357–82.

Carney, P. (2017). How does the photograph punish? In M. Brown and E. Carrabine (eds) *Routledge International Handbook of Visual Criminology*. Abingdon: Routledge, pp. 280–92.

Carrabine, E. (2010). Imagining prison: Culture, history, space. *Prison Service Journal*, 187, 15–22.

Carrabine, E. (2011). Images of torture: Culture, politics and power. *Crime, Media, Culture*, 7(1), 5–30.

Carrabine, E. (2012). Just images: Aesthetics, ethics and visual criminology. *The British Journal of Criminology*, 52(3), 463–89.

Carrabine, E. (2015). Visual criminology: History, theory, and method. In H. Copes and J.M. Miller (eds) *The Routledge Handbook of Qualitative Criminology*. Abingdon: Routledge, pp. 103–21.

Carrabine, E. (2016). Doing visual criminology. In M.H. Jacobsen and S. Walklate (eds) *Liquid Criminology: Doing Imaginative Criminological Research*. Abingdon: Routledge, pp. 121–39.

Carrabine, E. (2017). Social science and visual culture. In M. Brown and E. Carrabine (eds) *Routledge International Handbook of Visual Criminology*. Abingdon: Routledge, pp. 23–38.

Carrabine, E. (2019). Reading pictures: Piranesi and carceral landscapes. In J. Fleetwood, L. Presser, S. Sandberg, and T. Ugelvik (eds) *The Emerald Handbook of Narrative Criminology*. Bingley, UK: Emerald Group Publishing, pp. 197–216.

Cavender, G., Bond-Maupin, L. and Jurik, N.C. (1999). The construction of gender in reality crime TV. *Gender & Society*, 13(5), 643–63.

Chamayou, G. (2012). *Manhunts: A Philosophical History*. Princeton, NJ: Princeton University Press.

Chasnoff, I.J., Burns, W.J., Schnoll, S.H. and Burns, K.A. (1985). Cocaine use in pregnancy. *New England Journal of Medicine*, 313(11), 666–9.

Chermak, S. and Weiss, A. (2005). Maintaining legitimacy using external communication strategies: An analysis of police-media relations. *Journal of Criminal Justice*, 33(5), 501–12.

Cohen, S. (2013). *States of Denial: Knowing about Atrocities and Suffering*. Hoboken, NJ: John Wiley & Sons.

Collier, J. and Collier, M. (1967). *Visual Anthropology: Photography as a Research Method*. Albuquerque, NM: University of New Mexico Press.

Comaroff, J.A. and Comaroff, J. (2004). Criminal obsessions, after Foucault: Postcoloniality, policing, and the metaphysics of disorder. *Critical Inquiry*, 30(4), 800–24.

Cook, I.R. and Ashutosh, I. (2018). Television drama and the urban diegesis: Portraying Albuquerque in *Breaking Bad*. *Urban Geography*, 39(5), 746–62.

Copes, H., Tchoula, W., Kim, J. and Ragland, J. (2018a). Symbolic perceptions of methamphetamine: Differentiating between ice and shake. *International Journal of Drug Policy*, 51, 87–94.

Copes, H., Tchoula, W., Brookman, F. and Ragland, J. (2018b). Photo-elicitation interviews with vulnerable populations: Practical and ethical considerations. *Deviant Behavior*, 39(4), 475–94.

Copes, H., Tchoula, W. and Ragland, J. (2019). Ethically representing drug use: Photographs and ethnographic research with people who use methamphetamine. *Journal of Qualitative Criminal Justice & Criminology*, 8(1). https://doi.org/10.21428/88de04a1.2e48b8e5

Correia, D. and Wall, T. (2018). *Police: A Field Guide*. London: Verso Books.

Czerniak, J. (1997). Challenging the pictorial: Recent landscape practice. *Assemblage*, 34, 110–20.

Davis, A. (2003). *Are Prisons Obsolete?* New York, NY: Seven Stories.

Debord, G. (2008). *Introduction to a Critique of Urban Geography*. Glasgow: Praxis Press.

Debord, G. (2012). *Society of the Spectacle*. Bread and Circuses Publishing.

Deleuze, G. (1986). *Cinema 1: The Movement-Image* (trans. H. Tomlinson and B. Habberjam). Minneapolis, MN: University of Minnesota Press.

Deleuze, G. (2013). *Cinema II: The Time-Image*. London: Bloomsbury.

Delmas, M.A. and Burbano, V.C. (2011). The drivers of greenwashing. *California Management Review*, 54(1), 64–87.

Dirks, D. (2004). Sexual revictimization and retraumatization of women in prison. *Women's Studies Quarterly*, 32(3/4), 102–15.

Dirks, D., Heldman, C. and Zack, E. (2015). 'She's white and she's hot, so she can't be guilty': Female criminality, penal spectatorship, and white protectionism. *Contemporary Justice Review*, 18(2), 160–77.

Donloe, D. (1993). *Gordon Parks*. Los Angeles, CA: Holloway House Publishing.

Dubber, M.D. (2005). *The Police Power: Patriarchy and the Foundations of American Government*. New York, NY: Columbia University Press.

Duffy, L. (2011). 'Step-by-step we are stronger': Women's empowerment through photovoice. *Journal of Community Health Nursing*, 28(2), 105–16.

Dufour, D. and Delage, C. (eds) (2015). *Images of Conviction: The Construction of Visual Evidence*. Paris: Le Bal.

Dugdale, R.L. (1877). *' The Jukes': A Study in Crime, Pauperism, Diseases, and Heredity; Also, Further Studies of Criminals*. New York, NY: GP Putnam's sons.

Earle, R. (2018). Convict criminology in England: Developments and dilemmas. *The British Journal of Criminology*, 58(6), 1499–516.

Eigenberg, H.M. and Park, S. (2016). Marginalization and invisibility of women of color: A content analysis of race and gender images in introductory criminal justice and criminology texts. *Race and Justice*, 6(3), 257–79.

Evans, J. (2018). Photography as an ethics of seeing. In J. Evans, P. Betts, and S. Hoffman (eds) *The Ethics of Seeing: Photography and Twentieth-century German History*. New York, NY: Berghahn, pp. 1–21.

Fanon, F. (2016 [1952]). The fact of blackness. In P.K. Nayar (ed) *Postcolonial Studies: An Anthology*. Hoboken, NJ: John Wiley and Sons, pp. 15–32.

Farebrother, R. and Champkin, J. (2014). Alphonse Bertillon and the measure of man: More expert than Sherlock Holmes. *Significance*, 11(2), 36–9.

Ferrell, J. (1993). *Crimes of Style: Urban Graffiti and the Politics of Criminality*. New York, NY: Garland.

Ferrell, J. (1995). Urban graffiti: Crime, control, and resistance. *Youth & Society*, 27(1), 73–92.

Ferrell, J. (1997a). Youth, crime, and cultural space. *Social Justice*, 24(4), 21–38.

Ferrell, J. (1997b). Criminological verstehen: Inside the immediacy of crime. *Justice Quarterly*, 14(1), 3–23.

Ferrell, J. (1999). Cultural criminology. *Annual Review of Sociology*, 25(1), 395–418.

Ferrell, J. (2004). Boredom, crime and criminology. *Theoretical Criminology*, 8(3), 287–302.

Ferrell, J. (2007). For a ruthless cultural criticism of everything existing. *Crime, Media, Culture*, 3(1), 91–100.

Ferrell, J. (2009). Against method, against authority … for anarchy. In R. Amster, A. DeLeon, L. Fernandez, A. Nocella, and D. Shannon (eds) *Contemporary Anarchist Studies: An Anthology of Anarchy in the Academy*. Abingdon: Routledge, pp. 73–82.

Ferrell, J. (2013). Tangled up in green: Cultural criminology and green criminology. In N. South and A. Brisman (eds) *Routledge International Handbook of Green Criminology*. Abingdon: Routledge, pp. 349–64.

Ferrell, J. (2017). We never, never talked about photography. In M. Brown and E. Carrabine (eds) *Routledge International Handbook of Visual Criminology*. Abingdon, UK: Routledge, pp. 40–52.

Ferrell, J. (2019). In defense of resistance. *Critical Criminology*, 1–17. https://doi.org/10.1007/s10612-019-09456-6

Ferrell, J. and Van de Voorde, C. (2010). The decisive moment: Documentary photography and cultural criminology. In K. Hayward and M. Presdee (eds) *Framing Crime: Cultural Criminology and the Image*. Abingdon: Routledge, pp. 36–52.

Fiddler, M. (2007). Projecting the prison: The depiction of the uncanny in The Shawshank Redemption. *Crime, Media, Culture*, 3(2), 192–206.

Finn, J.M. (2009). *Capturing the Criminal Image: From Mug Shot to Surveillance Society*. Minneapolis, MN: University of Minnesota Press.

Fisher, J.A. (2001). High art versus low art. In B. Gault and D. Lopes (eds) *The Routledge Companion to Aesthetics*. Abingdon: Routledge, pp. 473–84.

Fisher, M. (2009). *Capitalist Realism: Is There No Alternative?* London: John Hunt Publishing.

Fitzgerald, J.L. (2002). Drug photography and harm reduction: Reading John Ranard. *International Journal of Drug Policy*, 13(5), 369–85.

Fitzgibbon, W. and Stengel, C.M. (2018). Women's voices made visible: Photovoice in visual criminology. *Punishment & Society*, 20(4), 411–31.

Fitzgibbon, W., Graebsch, C. and McNeill, F. (2017). Pervasive punishment: The shadow of penal supervision. In M. Brown and E. Carrabine (eds) *Routledge International Handbook of Visual Criminology*. Abingdon: Routledge, pp. 305–19.

Fleetwood, J., Presser, L., Sandberg, S., and Ugelvik, T. (eds) (2019). *The Emerald Handbook of Narrative Criminology*. Bingley, UK: Emerald Group Publishing.

Flores, M.I., Grineski, S.E. and Collins, T.W. (2011). Using visual images to achieve environmental justice: A case study of the Asarco Copper Smelter in El Paso, Texas. *Environmental Justice*, 4(1), 45–53.

Flynn, M. and Hall, M. (2017). The case for a victimology of nonhuman animal harms. *Contemporary Justice Review*, 20(3), 299–318.

Foucault, M. (1977). *Discipline and Punish* (trans. A. Sheridan). Paris: Gallimard.

Francis, D. (2012). *The Imaginary Indian: The Image of the Indian in Canadian Culture*. Vancouver: Arsenal Pulp Press.

Freeland, C. (2012). Aesthetics and the senses: Introduction. *Essays in Philosophy*, 13(2), 399–403.

Frost, N.A. (2010). Beyond public opinion polls: Punitive public sentiment & criminal justice policy. *Sociology Compass*, 4(3), 156–68.

Ghandnoosh, N. (2019). *U.S. Prison Population Trends: Massive Buildup and Modest Decline*. Report prepared for The Sentencing Project, available at www.sentencingproject.org/publications/ u-s-prison-population-trends-massive-buildup-and-modest-decline

Gilmore, R.W. (2002). Fatal couplings of power and difference: Notes on racism and geography. *The Professional Geographer*, 54(1), 15–24.

Gilmore, R.W. (2007). *Golden Gulag: Prisons, Surplus, Crisis, and Opposition in Globalizing California* (Vol. 21). Berkeley, CA: University of California Press.

Gilroy, P. (2000). *Against Race: Imagining Political Culture Beyond the Color Line*. Cambridge, MA: Harvard University Press.

Glazek, C. (2012). Raise the crime rate. *N+1*, 1(13), 1–8.

Glover, K.S. (2019). Identifying racialized knowledge through a critical race studies lens: Theory and principles for the criminology textbook realm. *Contemporary Justice Review*, 22(4), 371–88.

Goffman, E. (1959). *The Presentation of Self in Everyday Life*. London: Doubleday.

Goldsmith, A.J. (2010). Policing's new visibility. *The British Journal of Criminology*, 50(5), 914–34.

Gordon, A. (1997). *Ghostly Matters: Haunting and the Sociological Imagination*. Minneapolis, MN: University of Minnesota Press.

Goyes, D. and Sollund, R. (2016). Contesting and contextualising CITES: Wildlife trafficking in Colombia and Brazil. *International Journal for Crime, Justice and Social Democracy*, 5(4), 87–102.

Graham, D.W. (2007). Heraclitus. *Stanford Encyclopedia of Philosophy* [online], available at https://plato.stanford.edu/entries/heraclitus

Gross, L.P., Katz, J.S. and Ruby, J. (eds) (2003). *Image Ethics in the Digital Age*. Minneapolis, MN: University of Minnesota Press.

Hall, R. (2009). *Wanted: The Outlaw in American Visual Culture*. Charlottesville, VA: University of Virginia Press.

Hall, S. (1992). Race, culture, and communications: Looking backward and forward at cultural studies. *Rethinking Marxism*, 5(1), 10–18.

Hall, S., Critcher, C., Jefferson, T., Clarke, J. and Roberts, B. (1978). *Policing the Crisis: Mugging, the State, and Law and Order*. London: Macmillan.

Halsey, M. (2013). Conservation criminology and the 'General Accident' of climate change. In A. Brisman and N. South (eds) *The Routledge International Handbook of Green Criminology*. Abingdon: Routledge, pp. 107–19.

Halsey, M. and Young, A. (2002). The meanings of graffiti and municipal administration. *Australian & New Zealand Journal of Criminology*, 35(2), 165–86.

Halsey, M. and Young, A. (2006). 'Our desires are ungovernable': Writing graffiti in urban space. *Theoretical Criminology*, 10(3), 275–306.

Harper, D. (1988). Visual sociology: Expanding sociological vision. *The American Sociologist*, 19(1), 54–70.

Hayward, K. (2004). Space—the final frontier: Criminology, the city and the spatial dynamics of exclusion. In J. Ferrell, K. Hayward, W. Morrison and M. Presdee (eds) *Cultural Criminology Unleashed*. London: The Glass House Press, pp. 155–66.

Hayward, K. (2010). Opening the lens. In K. Hayward and M. Presdee (eds) *Framing Crime: Cultural Criminology and the Image*. Abingdon: Routledge, pp. 1–16.

Hayward, K. (2012). Five spaces of cultural criminology. *The British Journal of Criminology*, 52(3), 441–62.

Hayward, K. (2016a). The future of (spatial) criminology and research about public space. In M. De Backer, L. Melgaco, G. Varna, and F. Menichelli (eds) *Order and Conflict in Public Space*. Abingdon: Routledge, pp. 207–15.

Hayward, K. (2016b). *City Limits: Crime, Consumer Culture and the Urban Experience*. Abingdon: Routledge.

Hayward, K. (2016c). Cultural criminology: Script rewrites. *Theoretical Criminology*, 20(3), 297–321.

Hayward, K. (2017). Documentary criminology: A cultural criminological introduction. In M. Brown and E. Carrabine (eds) *Routledge International Handbook of Visual Criminology*. Abingdon: Routledge, pp. 135–50.

Hayward, K. and Presdee, M. (eds) (2010). *Framing Crime: Cultural Criminology and the Image*. Abingdon: Routledge.

Herbert, S. (1998). Police subculture reconsidered. *Criminology*, 36(2), 343–70.

Hippler, T. (2017). *Governing from the Skies: A Global History of Aerial Bombing*. London: Verso Books.

Hockings, P. (ed) (1999). *Principles of Visual Anthropology*. Berlin: Walter de Gruyter.

Holdaway, S. (1980). The police station. *Urban Life*, 9(1), 79–100.

Hope, M. (2020). Australia burning. *The Lancet Planetary Health*, 4(1), e12–e13.

Hudson, A. (2015). Beyond Homan Square: US history is steeped in torture. *Truthout*, 26 March, available at https://truthout.org/articles/beyond-homan-square-us-history-is-steeped-in-torture/

Huling, T. (2002). Building a prison economy in rural America. In M. Mauer and M. Chesney-Lind (eds) *Invisible Punishment: The Collateral Consequences of Mass Imprisonment*. New York, NY: The New Press, pp. 197–213.

Hutson, L. (2005). Rethinking the 'spectacle of the scaffold': Juridical epistemologies and English revenge tragedy. *Representations*, 89(1), 30–58.

Jay, M. (1988). The rise of hermeneutics and the crisis of ocularcentrism. *Poetics Today*, 9(2), 307–26.

Jay, M. (1991). The disenchantment of the eye: Surrealism and the crisis of ocularcentrism. *Visual Anthropology Review*, 7(1), 15–38.

Jay, M. (2002a). Cultural relativism and the visual turn. *Journal of Visual Culture*, 1(3), 267–78.

Jay, M. (2002b). That visual turn. *Journal of Visual Culture*, 1(1), 87–92.

Jewkes, Y. (2018). Just design: Healthy prisons and the architecture of hope. *Australian & New Zealand Journal of Criminology*, 51(3), 319–38.

Jewkes, Y. and Johnston, H. (2007). The evolution of prison architecture. In Y. Jewkes, J. Bennett, and B. Crewe (eds) *Handbook on Prisons*. Abingdon: Routledge, pp. 172–96.

Jewkes, Y. and Linnemann, T. (2017). *Media and Crime in the US*. Thousand Oaks, CA: Sage Publications.

Jewkes, Y. and Moran, D. (2017). Prison architecture and design: Perspectives from criminology and carceral geography. In A. Liebling, S. Maruna, and L. McAra (eds) *Oxford Handbook of Criminology* Oxford: Oxford University Press, pp. 541–61.

Johnson, H., South, N. and Walters, R. (2016). The commodification and exploitation of fresh water: Property, human rights and green criminology. *International Journal of Law, Crime and Justice*, 44, 146–62.

Johnson, J. (2011). 'The arithmetic of compassion': Rethinking the politics of photography. *British Journal of Political Science*, 41(3), 621–43.

Jones, A. (2003a). Introduction: Conceiving the intersection of feminism and visual culture. In A. Jones (ed) *The Feminism and Visual Culture Reader*. East Sussex: Psychology Press, pp. 1–7.

Jones, A. (ed) (2003b). *The Feminism and Visual Culture Reader*. East Sussex: Psychology Press.

Jovanović, A.V. (2004). Narratives in the visual field: Legacy of 1968 in Belgrade and the art of performance. *Belgrade English Language and Literature Studies*, IX, 183–97.

Katz, J. (1988). *Seductions of Crime: Moral and Sensual Attractions in Doing Evil*. New York, NY: Basic Books.

Kessi, S. (2011). Photovoice as a practice of re-presentation and social solidarity: Experiences from a youth empowerment project in Dar es Salaam and Soweto. *Papers on Social Representations*, 20(1), 7–1.

Khazam, O. (2014). *It's Right Under Your Nose!: The Trial of the Senses and the 'Plain Smell' Doctrine*. Montreal: Centre for Sensory Studies, Concordia University, available at http://centreforsensorystudies. org/occasional-papers/its-right-under-your-nose-the-trial-of-the-senses-and-the-plain-smell-doctrine

King, A. and Maruna, S. (2020). 'It is the sensual, stupid': Katz and the futures of criminology. In D. Polizzi (ed) *Jack Katz: Seduction, the Street and Emotion*. Bingley, UK: Emerald Publishing Limited, pp. 25–39.

Kilgore, J. (2016). E-carceration: The problematic world of being on an electric monitor. *AlterNet* [online], 20 October, available at www. alternet.org/2016/10/electronic-monitoring-restrictive-and-wrong

Kindynis, T. (2014). Ripping up the map: Criminology and cartography reconsidered. *The British Journal of Criminology*, 54(2), 222–43.

Kindynis, T. (2017). Urban exploration: From subterranea to spectacle. *The British Journal of Criminology*, 57(4), 982–1001.

King, R.S., Mauer, M. and Huling, T. (2003). *Big Prisons, Small Towns: Prison Economics in Rural America*. Washington, DC: Sentencing Project.

Kleinman, A. and Kleinman, J. (1996). The appeal of experience; the dismay of images: Cultural appropriations of suffering in our times. *Daedalus*, 125(1), 1–23.

Klimas, J., Gorfinkel, L., Fairbairn, N., Amato, L., Ahamad, K., Nolan, S., Simel, D., and Wood, E. (2019). Strategies to identify patient risks of prescription opioid addiction when initiating opioids for pain: A systematic review. *JAMA Network Open*, 2(5), e193365.

Klingender, F. (2019). *Animals in Art and Thought: To the End of the Middle Ages* (Vol. 28). Abingdon: Routledge.

Knauss, S. and Pezzoli-Olgiati, D. (2015). The normative power of images: Religion, gender, visuality. *Religion and Gender*, 5(1), 1–17.

Kohm, S.A. and Greenhill, P. (2011). Pedophile crime films as popular criminology: A problem of justice? *Theoretical Criminology*, 15(2), 195–215.

Kohm, S. and Greenhill, P. (2013). 'This is the north, where we do what we want': Popular green criminology and 'Little Red Riding Hood' films. In N. South and A. Brisman (eds) *Routledge International Handbook of Green Criminology*. Abingdon: Routledge, pp. 365–78.

Ladner, J.A. (ed) (1998). *The Death of White Sociology: Essays on Race and Culture*. Baltimore, MD: Black Classic Press.

Lam, A. (2021). Decoding the crime scene photograph: Seeing and narrating the death of a gangster. *International Journal for the Semiotics of Law/Revue internationale de Sémiotique juridique*, 34, 1–18.

Lam, A. and Tegelberg, M. (2020). *Criminal Anthroposcenes in the Vanishing Arctic*. London: Palgrave.

Lashmar, P. (2014). How to humiliate and shame: A reporter's guide to the power of the mugshot. *Social Semiotics*, 24(1), 56–87.

Lee, M. and McGovern, A. (2013). Image work(s): The new police (popularity) culture. In K. Carrington, M. Ball, E. O'Brien, and J. Tauri (eds) *Crime, Justice and Social Democracy*. London: Palgrave Macmillan, pp. 120–32.

Lee, S.E. (1954). Chinese landscape painting. *The Bulletin of the Cleveland Museum of Art*, 41(9), 199–201.

Lewis, S. (2019). The racial bias built into photography. *The New York Times*, 25 April, available at www.nytimes.com/2019/04/25/lens/sarah-lewis-racial-bias-photography.html

Linnemann, T. (2013). Governing through meth: Local politics, drug control and the drift toward securitization. *Crime, Media, Culture*, 9(1), 39–61.

Linnemann, T. (2016). *Meth Wars: Police, Media, Power*. New York, NY: NYU Press.

Linnemann, T. (2017a). Proof of death: Police power and the visual economies of seizure, accumulation and trophy. *Theoretical Criminology*, 21(1), 57–77.

Linnemann, T. (2017b). In plain view: Violence and the police image. In M. Brown and E. Carrabine (eds) *Routledge International Handbook of Visual Criminology*. Abingdon: Routledge, pp. 243–54.

Linnemann, T. and Kurtz, D.L. (2014). Beyond the ghetto: Police power, methamphetamine and the rural war on drugs. *Critical Criminology*, 22(3), 339–55.

Linnemann, T. and Medley, C. (2019). Black sites, 'dark sides': War power, police power, and the violence of the (un)known. *Crime, Media, Culture*, 15(2), 341–58.

Linnemann, T. and Wall, T. (2013). 'This is your face on meth': The punitive spectacle of 'white trash' in the rural war on drugs. *Theoretical Criminology*, 17(3), 315–34.

Linnemann, T., Hanson, L. and Williams, L.S. (2013). 'With scenes of blood and pain': Crime control and the punitive imagination of the meth project. *The British Journal of Criminology*, 53(4), 605–23.

Lippens, R. (2010). Law, code and late modern governance in prophetic painting: Notes on Jackson Pollock, Mark Rothko and Gilles Deleuze. In A. Wagner and J. Broekman (eds) *Prospects of Legal Semiotics*. Dordrecht: Springer, pp. 171–92.

Loader, I. and Sparks, R. (2011) *Public Criminology?* Abingdon: Routledge.

Logan, E. (1999). The wrong race, committing crime, doing drugs, and maladjusted for motherhood: The nation's fury over 'crack babies'. *Social Justice*, 26(1), 115–38.

Lynch, M.J. (1990). The greening of criminology: A perspective on the 1990s. *Critical Criminologist*, 2(3–4), 165–9.

Lyons, P. and Rittner, B. (1998). The construction of the crack babies phenomenon as a social problem. *American Journal of Orthopsychiatry*, 68(2), 313–20.

MacIndoe, G. (2018). 'As a recovering addict, I know those pictures live forever.' *Nieman Reports*, Winter, available at https://nieman. harvard.edu/articles/images-of-addiction-and-recovery/

Margolis, E. (1999). Class pictures: Representations of race, gender and ability in a century of school photography. *Visual Studies*, 14(1), 7–38.

Mawby, R.C. (2001). Promoting the police? The rise of police image work. *Criminal Justice Matters*, 43(1), 44–5.

McClanahan, B. (2014). Green and grey: Water justice, criminalization, and resistance. *Critical Criminology*, 22(3), 403–18.

McClanahan, B. (2016). Pollution, access, and binary division: Water activism and a human right to water. In T. Wyatt (ed) *Hazardous Waste and Pollution*. Cham: Springer, pp. 63–78.

McClanahan, B. (2017). Capturing Appalachia: Visualizing coal, culture, and ecology. Doctoral dissertation, University of Essex.

McClanahan, B. (2019). Earth–world–planet: Rural ecologies of horror and dark green criminology. *Theoretical Criminology*. https://doi.org/ 10.1177/1362480618819813

McClanahan, B. and Brisman, A. (2015). Climate change and peacemaking criminology: Ecophilosophy, peace and security in the 'war on climate change'. *Critical Criminology*, 23(4), 417–31.

McClanahan, B. and Brisman, A. (2016). Police violence and the failed promise of human rights. In L. Weber, E. Fishwick and M. Marmo (eds) *The Routledge International Handbook of Criminology and Human Rights*. Abingdon: Routledge, pp. 359–67.

McClanahan, B. and Linnemann, T. (2018). Darkness on the edge of town: Visual criminology and the 'black sites' of the rural. *Deviant Behavior*, 39(4), 512–24.

McClanahan, B. and South, N. (2020). 'All knowledge begins with the senses': Towards a sensory criminology. *The British Journal of Criminology*, 60(1), 3–23.

McClanahan, B., Brisman, A and South, N. (2017). Green criminology, culture, and cinema. In *Oxford Research Encyclopedia of Criminology and Criminal Justice* [online], available at https://doi.org/10.1093/acrefore/9780190264079.013.151

McGoey, L. (2012). The logic of strategic ignorance. *The British Journal of Sociology*, 63(3), 533–76.

McGregor, R. (2020). *A Criminology of Narrative Fiction*. Bristol, UK: Policy Press.

McKay, C. and Lee, M. (2020). Body-worn images: Point-of-view and the new aesthetics of policing. *Crime, Media, Culture*, 16(3), 431–50.

McLuhan, M. and Fiore, Q. (1967). The medium is the message. *New York*, 123, 126–8.

McNatt, G. (2004). Conscience of artist is missing in photos. *The Baltimore Sun*, 2 December, available at https://www.baltimoresun.com/news/bs-xpm-2004-12-02-0412020207-story.html

Millie, A. (2012). Police stations, architecture and public reassurance. *The British Journal of Criminology*, 52(6), 1092–112.

Millie, A. (2017). Urban interventionism as a challenge to aesthetic order: Towards an aesthetic criminology. *Crime, Media, Culture*, 13(1), 3–20.

Millie, A. (2019). Crimes of the senses: Yarn bombing and aesthetic criminology. *The British Journal of Criminology*, 59(6), 1269–87.

Mills, C.W. (1959). *The Sociological Imagination*. Oxford: Oxford University Press.

Mirzoeff, N. (2011a). *The Right to Look: A Counterhistory of Visuality*. Durham NC: Duke University Press.

Mirzoeff, N. (2011b). The right to look. *Critical Inquiry*, 37(3), 473–96.

Mitchell, W.T. (2005). *What do Pictures Want? The Lives and Loves of Images*. Chicago, IL: University of Chicago Press.

Moran, D. (2015). *Carceral Geography: Spaces and Practices of Incarceration*. Farnham: Ashgate.

Morrison, W. (2004). Lombroso and the birth of criminological positivism: Scientific mastery or cultural artifice. In J. Ferrell, K. Hayward, W. Morrison and M. Presdee (eds) *Cultural Criminology Unleashed*. London: The Glass House Press, pp. 67–80.

Morton, T. (2018). *Being Ecological*. Cambridge, MA: MIT Press.

Moten, F. (2008). The case of blackness. *Criticism*, 50(2), 177–218.

Mulcahy, L. (2015). Docile suffragettes? Resistance to police photography and the possibility of object–subject transformation. *Feminist Legal Studies*, 23(1), 79–99.

Mulvey, L. (1989). *Visual and Other Pleasures*. New York, NY: Springer.

Naegler, L. (2012). *Gentrification and Resistance: Cultural Criminology, Control, and the Commodification of Urban Protest in Hamburg* (Vol. 50). Münster: LIT Verlag.

Nakamura, L. (2008). *Digitizing Race: Visual Cultures of the Internet* (Vol. 23). Minneapolis, MN: University of Minnesota Press.

Natali, L. (2010). The big grey elephants in the backyard of Huelva, Spain. In R. White (ed) *Global Environmental Harm: Criminological Perspectives*. Abingdon: Routledge, pp. 193–209.

Natali, L. (2013). The contemporary horizon of green criminology. In N. South and A. Brisman (eds) *Routledge International Handbook of Green Criminology*. Abingdon: Routledge, pp. 73–84.

Natali, L. (2016). *A Visual Approach for Green Criminology: Exploring the Social Perception of Environmental Harm*. New York, NY: Springer.

Natali, L and McClanahan, B. (2017). Perceiving and communicating environmental contamination and change: Towards a green cultural criminology with images. *Critical Criminology*, 25(2), 199–214.

Natali, L. and McClanahan, B. (2020). The visual dimensions of green criminology. In N. South and A. Brisman (eds) *Routledge International Handbook of Green Criminology* (2nd edn). Abingdon: Routledge, pp. 95–107.

Neocleous, M. (2000). *The Fabrication of Social Order: A Critical Theory of Police Power*. London: Pluto Press.

Neocleous, M. (2014). *War Power, Police Power*. Edinburgh: Edinburgh University Press.

Neocleous, M., Rigakos, G., and Wall, T. (2013). On pacification: Introduction to the special issue. *Socialist Studies/Études socialistes*, 9(2), 1–6.

Neumann, R.P. (2003). The production of nature: Colonial recasting of the African landscape in Serengeti National Park. In K. Zimmerer and T. Bassett (eds) *Political ecology: An integrative approach to geography and environment-development studies*, New York, NY: The Guildford Press, pp 240–55.

Norton, J. and Kang-Brown, J. (2020). If you build it: How the federal government fuels rural jail expansion. Vera Institute of Justice [online], available at www.vera.org/in-our-backyards-stories/if-you-build-it

Nurse, A. (2014). Cleaning up greenwash: The case for enforcing corporate environmental responsibility. *Internet Journal of Criminology*, 90–107.

Nurse, A. (2015). *Policing Wildlife: Perspectives on the Enforcement of Wildlife Legislation*. Basingstoke: Palgrave Macmillan.

Paglen, T. (2010). *Blank Spots on the Map: The Dark Geography of the Pentagon's Secret World*. London: Penguin.

Park, S.M., Kim, J.L., Park, H., Kim, Y. and Cuadrado, M. (2018). Social constructions of racial images in introductory criminal justice and criminology textbooks: A content analysis. *Race Ethnicity and Education*, 1–14. DOI: 10.1080/13613324.2018.1538122

Patten, D. (2016). The mass incarceration of nations and the global war on drugs: Comparing the United States' domestic and foreign drug policies. *Social Justice*, 43(1), 85–105.

Pauwels, L. (2000). Taking the visual turn in research and scholarly communication key issues in developing a more visually literate (social) science. *Visual Studies*, 15(1), 7–14.

Pauwels, L. (2011). An integrated conceptual framework for visual social research. In E. Margolis and L. Pauwels (eds) *The SAGE Handbook of Visual Research Methods*. Newbury Park, CA: SAGE.

Pauwels, L. (2015). *Reframing Visual Social Science: Towards a More Visual Sociology and Anthropology*. Cambridge: Cambridge University Press.

Pensky, M. (2004). Method and time: Benjamin's dialectical images. In D. Ferris (ed) *The Cambridge Companion to Walter Benjamin*. Cambridge: Cambridge University Press, pp. 177–98.

Phelan, M.P. and Hunt, S.A. (1998). Prison gang members' tattoos as identity work: The visual communication of moral careers. *Symbolic Interaction*, 21(3), 277–98.

Pink, S. (2020). *Doing Visual Ethnography*. London: Sage.

Plant, S. (2002). *The Most Radical Gesture: The Situationist International in a Postmodern Age*. Abingdon: Routledge.

Presser, L. and Sandberg, S. (eds) (2015). *Narrative Criminology: Understanding Stories of Crime* (Vol. 17). New York, NY: NYU Press.

Price, M.E. (2005). Punitive sentiment among the Shuar and in industrialized societies: Cross-cultural similarities. *Evolution and Human Behavior*, 26(3), 279–87.

Rafter, N. (2005). Cesare Lombroso and the origins of criminology: Rethinking criminological tradition. *Publifarum*, 1, 6-6.

Rafter, N. (2007). Crime, film and criminology: Recent sex-crime movies. *Theoretical Criminology*, 11(3), 403–20.

Rafter, N. (2014). Introduction to special issue on visual culture and the iconography of crime and punishment. *Theoretical Criminology*, 18(2), 127–33.

Rafter, N. (2017). Crime films and visual criminology. In M. Brown and E. Carrabine (eds) *Routledge International Handbook of Visual Criminology*. Abingdon: Routledge, pp. 53–61.

Rafter, N.H. (ed) (1988). *White Trash: The Eugenic Family Studies, 1877–1919*. Boston, MA: Northeastern University Press.

Rafter, N.H. and Brown, M. (2011). *Criminology Goes to the Movies: Crime Theory and Popular Culture*. New York, NY: NYU Press.

Rafter, N. and Ystehede, P. (2010). Here be dragons: Lombroso, the gothic, and social control. In M. Deflem (ed) *Popular Culture, Crime and Social Control*. Bingley, UK: Emerald Group Publishing Limited, pp. 263–84.

Ramirez, M.D. (2013). Punitive sentiment. *Criminology*, 51(2), 329–64.

Rancière, J. (2009). Notes on the photographic image. *Radical Philosophy*, 156, 8–15.

Rancière, J. (2013). *Aisthesis: Scenes from the Aesthetic Regime of Art*. London: Verso Books.

Rancière, J. (2015). *Dissensus: On Politics and Aesthetics*. London: Bloomsbury.

Razack, S. (ed) (2002). *Race, Space, and the Law: Unmapping a White Settler Society*. Toronto: Between the Lines Books.

Razack, S. (2004). *Dark Threats and White Knights: The Somalia Affair, Peacekeeping, and the New Imperialism*. Toronto: University of Toronto Press.

Redmon, D. (2015). Documentary criminology: Expanding the criminological imagination with 'Mardi Gras—Made in China' as a case study (23 minutes). *Societies*, 5(2), 425–41.

Redmon, D. (2017). Documentary criminology: Girl Model as a case study. *Crime, Media, Culture*, 13(3), 357–74.

Redmon, D. (2018). Video methods, green cultural criminology, and the anthropocene: SANCTUARY as a case study. *Deviant Behavior*, 39(4), 495–511.

Revier, K. (2020). 'Now you're connected': Carceral visuality and police power on MobilePatrol. *Theoretical Criminology*, 24(2), 314–34.

Rigakos, G.S. (2011). 'To extend the scope of productive labour': Pacification as a police project. In M. Neocleous and G.S Rigakos (eds) *Anti-Security*. Ottawa: Red Quill Books, pp. 57–83.

Rigakos, G.S. (2016). *Security/Capital: A General Theory of Pacification*. Edinburgh: Edinburgh University Press.

Rodriguez, D. (2006). (Non)scenes of captivity: The common sense of punishment and death. *Radical History Review*, 96, 9–32.

Roth, L. (2009). Looking at Shirley, the ultimate norm: Colour balance, image technologies, and cognitive equity. *Canadian Journal of Communication*, 34(1), 111–36.

Rukavina, K. (2013). 'Ocularcentrism' or the privilege of sight in Western culture. The analysis of the concept in ancient, modern, and postmodern thought. *Filozofska istraživanja*, 32(3–4), 539–56.

Russell, E.K. (2017). A 'fair cop': Queer histories, affect and police image work in Pride March. *Crime, Media, Culture*, 13(3), 277–93.

Russell, E.K. (2020). Carceral atmospheres on Manus Island: Listening to how are you today. *Law Text Culture, 24*(1), 5.

Russell, E.K. and Rae, M. (2020). Indefinite stuckness: Listening in a time of hyper-incarceration and border entrapment. *Punishment & Society*, 22(3), 281–301.

Sagatun-Edwards, I.J. (1998). Crack babies, moral panic, and the criminalization of behavior during pregnancy. In E. Jensen and J. Gerber (eds) *The New War on Drugs: Symbolic Politics and Criminal Justice Policy*. Greenblet, MD: Academy of Criminal Justice Sciences, pp. 107–21.

Saleh-Hanna, V. (2017). Reversing criminology's white gaze: As Lombroso's disembodied head peers through a glass jar in a museum foreshadowed by Sara Baartman's ghost. In J. Wilson, S. Hodgkinson, J. Piché, and K. Walby (eds) *The Palgrave Handbook of Prison Tourism*. London: Palgrave Macmillan, pp. 689–711.

Saner, E. (2016). Just say no! What really happened when Grange Hill met Nancy Reagan at the White House. *The Guardian* [online], 27 March, available at www.theguardian.com/tv-and-radio/shortcuts/2016/mar/07/grange-hill-nancy-reagan-white-house-just-say-no

Schept, J. (2013). 'A lockdown facility … with the feel of a small, private college': Liberal politics, jail expansion, and the carceral habitus. *Theoretical Criminology*, 17(1), 71–88.

Schept, J. (2014). (Un)seeing like a prison: Counter-visual ethnography of the carceral state. *Theoretical Criminology*, 18(2), 198–223.

Schept, J. (2015). *Progressive Punishment: Job Loss, Jail Growth, and the Neoliberal Logic of Carceral Expansion* (Vol. 1). New York, NY: NYU Press.

Schept, J. and Frank, J. (2015). Challenging prison progress: Landscape and the dialectical image. *Crime Media Culture*, 11(1), 85–6.

Schneider, C.J. (2018). Body worn cameras and police image work: News media coverage of the Rialto police department's body worn camera experiment. *Crime, Media, Culture*, 14(3), 449–66.

Scott, J.C. (1990). *Domination and the Arts of Resistance: Hidden Transcripts*. New Haven, CT: Yale University Press.

Schrader, S. (2020). Wanted: An end to police terror. *Viewpoint Magazine* [online], 9 June, available at www.viewpointmag.com/2020/06/09/wanted-an-end-to-police-terror

Scott, J. and Staines, Z. (2020). Charting the place of islands in criminology: On isolation, integration and insularity. *Theoretical Criminology*, https://doi.org/10.1177/1362480620910250

Sekula, A. (1986). The body and the archive. Essay [online], October, 39(Winter), 3–64.

Self, W. (2007). *Psychogeography: Disentangling the Modern Conundrum of Psyche and Place*. London: Bloomsbury.

Semple, J. (1993). *Bentham's Prison: A Study of the Panopticon Penitentiary: A Study of the Panopticon Penitentiary*. Oxford: Oxford University Press.

Sharkey, J. (1993). When pictures drive foreign policy. *American Journalism Review*, 15(10), 14–20.

Siff, S. (2015). *Acid Hype: American News Media and the Psychedelic Experience*. Champaign, IL: University of Illinois Press.

Simon, J. (2001). Governing through crime metaphors. *Brooklyn Law Review*, 67(4), 1035–70.

Simon, J. (2007). *Governing Through Crime: How the War on Crime Transformed American Democracy and Created a Culture of Fear*. Oxford: Oxford University Press.

Skibins, J.C., Powell, R.B. and Hallo, J.C. (2013). Charisma and conservation: Charismatic megafauna's influence on safari and zoo tourists' pro-conservation behaviors. *Biodiversity and Conservation*, 22(4), 959–82.

Skilbrei, M.L. (2013). Sisters in crime: Representations of gender and class in the media coverage and court proceedings of the triple homicide at Orderud Farm. *Crime, Media, Culture*, 9(2), 136–52.

Small, R. (2015). Trevor Paglen dives deep. *Interview Magazine* [online], 17 September, available at www.interviewmagazine.com/art/trevor-paglen-metro-pictures

Smith, C. (2013). Spaces of punitive violence. *Criticism*, 55(1): 161–8.

Smith, S.M. (2004). *Photography on the Color Line: WEB Du Bois, Race, and Visual Culture*. Chapel Hill, NC: Duke University Press.

Smith, S.M. (2013). *At the Edge of Sight: Photography and the Unseen*. Chapel Hill, NC: Duke University Press.

Snyder, G.J. (2006). Graffiti media and the perpetuation of an illegal subculture. *Crime, Media, Culture*, 2(1), 93–101.

Snyder, G.J. (2011). *Graffiti Lives: Beyond the Tag in New York's Urban Underground* (Vol. 21). New York, NY: NYU Press.

Sollund, R. (2013). Animal trafficking and trade: Abuse and species injustice. In D. Westerhuis, R. Walters, and T. Wyatt (eds) *Emerging Issues in Green Criminology*. Palgrave Macmillan, London, pp. 72–92.

Sollund, R.A. (2019). *The Crimes of Wildlife Trafficking: Issues of Justice, Legality and Morality*. Abingdon: Routledge.

Sontag, S. (1977). *On Photography*. New York, NY: Farrar, Strauss and Giroux.

South, N. (1998). A green field for criminology? A proposal for a perspective. *Theoretical Criminology*, 2(2), 211–33.

Starks, M. (2015). *Cocaine Fiends and Reefer Madness: An Illustrated History of Drugs in the Movies 1894-1978*. Berkeley, CA: Ronin Publishing.

Story, B. (2017). Against a 'humanizing' prison cinema: *The Prison in Twelve Landscapes* and the politics of abolition imagery. In M. Brown and E. Carrabine (eds) *Routledge International Handbook of Visual Criminology*. Abingdon: Routledge, pp. 455–65.

Tagg, J. (1982). The currency of the photograph. In V. Burgin (ed) *Thinking Photography*. Basingstoke: Macmillan, pp. 110–41.

Tagg, J. (1993). *The Burden of Representation: Essays on Photographies and Histories* (Vol. 80). Minneapolis, MN: University of Minnesota Press.

Talbot, W.H.F. (1989). *The Pencil of Nature* (Vol. 1). Alexandria: Library of Alexandria.

Taylor, G.F. (2015). Chicago's Homan Square: Torture by any other name. *Huffington Post* [online], 17 March, available at www.huffpost.com/entry/chicago-homan-square-tort_b_6843750

Taylor, J., Dworin, J., Buell, B., Sepinuck, T., Palidofsky, M., Tofteland, C., ... and Wilcox, A. (2010). *Performing New Lives: Prison Theatre*. London: Jessica Kingsley Publishers.

Thompson, J.B. (2005). The new visibility. *Theory, Culture & Society*, 22(6), 31–51.

Tin, D., Hertelendy, A.J. and Ciottone, G.R. (2020). What we learned from the 2019–2020 Australian bushfire disaster: Making counter-terrorism medicine a strategic preparedness priority. *American Journal of Emergency Medicine*. Available online ahead of print. DOI: 10.1016/j.ajem.2020.09.069.

Turner, J. (2019). 'It all started with Eddie': Thanatopolitics, police power, and the murder of Edward Byrne. *Crime, Media, Culture*, 15(2), 239–58.

Twomey, C. (2012). Framing atrocity: Photography and humanitarianism. *History of Photography*, 36(3), 255–64.

Valier, C. and Lippens, R. (2004). Moving images, ethics and justice. *Punishment & Society*, 6(3), 319–33.

Van de Voorde, C. (2012). Ethnographic photography in criminological research. In D. Gadd, S. Karstedt, and S. Messner (eds) *The SAGE Handbook of Criminological Research Methods*. Newbury Park, CA: SAGE, pp. 203–17.

Vimalassery, M. (2016). Fugitive decolonization. *Theory & Event*, 19(4).

Wakeman, S. (2014). 'No one wins. One side just loses more slowly': *The Wire* and drug policy. *Theoretical Criminology*, 18(2), 224–40.

Wakeman, S. (2018). The 'one who knocks' and the 'one who waits': Gendered violence in *Breaking Bad*. *Crime, Media, Culture*, 14(2), 213–28.

Walker, H.L., Thorpe, R.U., Christensen, E.K. and Anderson, J.P. (2017). The hidden subsidies of rural prisons: Race, space and the politics of cumulative disadvantage. *Punishment & Society*, 19(4), 393–416.

Walklate, S. (2018). 'Seeing' gender, war and terror. *Criminology & Criminal Justice*, 18(5), 617–30.

Wall, T. (2013). Unmanning the police manhunt: Vertical security as pacification. *Socialist Studies/Études Socialistes*, 9(2), 32–56.

Wall, T. (2016). Ordinary emergency: Drones, police, and geographies of legal terror. *Antipode*, 48(4), 1122–39.

Wall, T. (2019). The police invention of humanity: Notes on the 'thin blue line'. *Crime, Media, Culture*. https://doi.org/10.1177/1741659019873757

Wall, T. and Linnemann, T. (2014). Staring down the state: Police power, visual economies, and the 'war on cameras'. *Crime, Media, Culture*, 10(2), 133–49.

Wall, T. and McClanahan, B. (2015). Weaponising conservation in the 'heart of darkness': The war on poachers and the neocolonial hunt. In A. Brisman, N. South, and R. White (eds) *Environmental Crime and Social Conflict: Contemporary and Emerging Issues*. Abingdon: Routledge, pp. 221–40.

Wall, T., Saberi, P. and Jackson, W. (eds) (2017). *Destroy, Build, Secure: Readings on Pacification*. Ottawa: Red Quill Books.

Wang, C. and Burris, M.A. (1997). Photovoice: Concept, methodology, and use for participatory needs assessment. *Health Education & Behavior*, 24(3), 369–87.

Webster, L.R. (2013). Pills, polices, and predicaments: The unintended consequences of a health care system's policy toward opioids. *Pain Medicine*, 14(10), 1439–40.

West, K. (2017). Visual criminology and Lombroso: In memory of Nicole Rafter (1939–2016). *Theoretical Criminology*, 21(3), 271–87.

West, K. (2019). What was criminology? From photography to painting in Cesare Lombroso's (1835–1909) criminal anthropology. Doctoral dissertation, University of Oxford.

White, R. (ed) (2012a). *Climate Change from a Criminological Perspective*. New York, NY: Springer.

White, R. (2012b). The criminology of climate change. In R. White (ed) *Climate Change from a Criminological Perspective*. New York, NY: Springer, pp. 1–11.

White, R. (2018a). *Climate Change Criminology*. Bristol: Policy Press.

White, R. (2018b). Green victimology and non-human victims. *International Review of Victimology*, 24(2), 239–55.

White, R. and Kramer, R.C. (2015). Critical criminology and the struggle against climate change ecocide. *Critical Criminology*, 23(4), 383–99.

Williams, R. (1976). *Keywords: A Vocabulary of Culture and Society*. Oxford: Oxford University Press.

Wilson, C.P. (2000). *Cop Knowledge: Police Power and Cultural Narrative in Twentieth-Century America*. Chicago, IL: University of Chicago Press.

Wilson, N., Dasho, S., Martin, A.C., Wallerstein, N., Wang, C.C. and Minkler, M. (2007). Engaging young adolescents in social action through photovoice: The youth empowerment strategies (YES!) project. *The Journal of Early Adolescence*, 27(2), 241–61.

Wood, S. (2016). Police body cameras: Emotional mediation and the economies of visuality. In S. Tettegah and S. Noble (eds) *Emotions, Technology, and Design*. Cambridge, MA: Academic Press, pp. 227–39.

Woods, B. (2018). Diarrhea diaries and dead drug dealers: The dangerous rhetoric and imagery of 'the opioid crisis'. *Isthmus* [online], 6 March, available at https://isthmus.com/opinion/democracy-in-crisis/diarrhea-diaries-and-dead-drug-dealers

Wyatt, T. (2012). *Green Criminology & Wildlife Trafficking: The Illegal Fur and Falcon Trades in Russia Far East*. Saarbrücken: Lambert Academic Publishing.

Wyatt, T. (2013). *Wildlife Trafficking: A Deconstruction of the Crime, the Victims, and the Offenders*. Basingstoke: Palgrave Macmillan.

Yar, M. (2012). Critical criminology, critical theory and social harm. In S. Hall and S. Winlow (eds) *New Directions in Criminological Theory*. Abingdon: Routledge, pp. 52–65.

Young, A. (2005). *Judging the Image: Art, Value, Law*. Abingdon: Routledge.

Young, A. (2012). Criminal images: The affective judgment of graffiti and street art. *Crime, Media, Culture*, 8(3), 297–314.

Young, A. (2014). From object to encounter: Aesthetic politics and visual criminology. *Theoretical Criminology*, 18(2), 159–75.

Yu, P., Xu, R., Abramson, M.J., Li, S. and Guo, Y. (2020). Bushfires in Australia: a serious health emergency under climate change. *The Lancet Planetary Health*, 4(1), e7–e8.

Zack, E., Lang, J.T. and Dirks, D. (2018). 'It must be great being a female pedophile!': The nature of public perceptions about female teacher sex offenders. *Crime, Media, Culture*, 14(1), 61–79.

Zillmann, D., Gibson, R. and Sargent, S.L. (1999). Effects of photographs in news-magazine reports on issue perception. *Media Psychology*, 1(3), 207–28.

Zimring, C.A. (2017). *Clean and White: A History of Environmental Racism in the United States*. New York, NY: New York University Press.

Index

References to figures are in *italics*. References to notes are the page number followed by the note number. Where there are duplicate note numbers on a page, the relevant chapter is given.

CPSIA information can be obtained
at www.ICGtesting.com
Printed in the USA
JSHW022343121222
34811JS00003B/42

9 781529 207453